Trudeau

The Life, Times and Passing of Pierre Elliott

TRUDEAU

National Post, The Montreal Gazette, Ottawa Citizen

Introduction by Roy MacGregor

KEY PORTER  BOOKS

Acknowledgements

The publisher is grateful to *National Post* review editor John Geiger for his work assembling and editing the various special sections on Pierre Elliott Trudeau, from which the following articles are excerpted. Thanks to Roy MacGregor for selecting, editing and contributing to the book. Denis Paquin of the *National Post* handled the photographs, along with Julie Nicholson, Brian Kerrigan, Andrew Tolson, Lyle Stafford, Alain-Pierre Hovasse. Thanks also to Scott Maniquet, Allison McLean and Siobhan Roberts.

Canadian Cataloguing in Publication Data available on request
ISBN 1-55263-336-5

THE CANADA COUNCIL | LE CONSEIL DES ARTS
FOR THE ARTS | DU CANADA
SINCE 1957 | DEPUIS 1957

The publisher gratefully acknowledges the support of the Canada Council for the Arts and the Ontario Arts Council for its publishing program.

We acknowledge the financial support of the Government of Canada through the Book Publishing Industry Development Program (BPIDP) for our publishing activities.

Key Porter Books Limited
70 The Esplanade
Toronto, Ontario
Canada M5E 1R2

www.keyporter.com

A portion of the proceeds from the sale of this book will be donated to prostate cancer research.

Cover and text design: Counterpunch/Linda Gustafson and Peter Ross

Printed and bound in Canada
00 01 02 03 04 05   6 5 4 3 2 1

Photo credits

Every effort has been made to contact copyright holders. In the event of omission or error the publisher should be notified. All photos: clockwise from top left. 1. CP photo/Ryan Remiorz; 2. CP photo/Chuck Mitchell; 3. CP photo/Ted Grant; 4. Andy Clark ;5. CP photo/Fred Chrantrand; 6. CP photo/Peter Bregg; 9. Robert Galbraith/National Post; 15. AFP photo/Dave Chan; 18. CP photo/Adrian Wyld; 19. Carlo Allegri/National Post; 20. Shaun Best/Reuters; CP photo/Adrian Wyld; 21. Carlo Allegri/National Post; CP photo/Jonathan Hayward; Chris Mikula/The Ottawa Citizen 22. Carlo Allegri/National Post; CP photo/Andrew Vaughan; 23. AFP photo/Jeff Kowalsky; 28. CP photo/Paul Chiasson; 29. NA 30. National Archives of Canada; 33. CP photo/Paul Chiasson; Shaun Best; 34. by Rod MacIvor; Andy Clark; CP photo/Peter Bregg; 35. Ottawa Citzen/Bruno Schlumberger; 36. Rod MacIvor/Ottawa; 39. CP photo; 40. National Archives of Canada; 42. Montreal Star photo, Taillefer; 43. National Archives of Canada; 44. National Archives of Canada; 46. CP photo/Joe Hourigan; 47. CP photo/AP; 49. CP; 50. CP photo/Ron Poling; 52.National Archives of Canada; 55. CP photo/Fred Chartrand; 56. Peter Jones/Reuters; CP; 57. CP photo/Ron Poling; CP photo/Chuck Mitchell; 58. CP photo/Peter Bregg; Leonard LePage/The Standard; CP photo/Ron Poling; 59. Gary Hershorn; CP photo/Chuck Mitchell; 60. Jim Young; 62. Patrick Doyle, Ottawa Citizen; 63. Vancouver Sun; 65. CP photo/Adrian Wyld; 67. CP photo/Adrian Wyld; 68. CP photo; 69. CP photo/Ron Poling; 70. Andy Clark; National Archives of Canada; 71. CP photo; CP photo/Fred Chartrand; CP photo/ Peter Bregg; 72. CP photo/Doug Ball; Andy Clark; CP photo/AP Scott Stewart ;CP photo/Peter Bregg; Rod MacIvor/Ottawa; 73. CP photo/Chuck Mitchell; CP photo; CP photo/Ron Bell; CP; 74. Drew Gragg, UPC; Rod MacIvor/Ottawa; 75. CP photo/Staff; NA; CP photo/Peter Bregg; 76. CP photo/Paul Chiasson; 77. Montreal Le Devoir-Jacques Grenier; 78. The Gazette; 80. Lynn Ball/The Ottawa Citizen; 83. CP photo/Doug Ball; 87. CP photo; 89. National Archives of Canada; 90. CP photo/Chuck Mitchell; CP photo; 93. National Archives of Canada; 94. CP photo/Peter Bregg; 95. CP photo/Chris Schwarz; 96. CP photo/Paul Chiasson; 97. CP 99. Robert Galbraith / National Post; 100. CP photo/Paul Chiasson; 101. Andy Clark; 102. Andy Clark; 103. The Daily Gleanor/Bob Wilson; 104. CP photo/ Tom Hanson; CP photo/Ryan Remiorz; John Major/Ottawa Citizen; 105. CP photo/Ryan Remiorz; 108. CP photo/Peter Bregg; 111. Vancouver Province; Vancouver Province/Bill Cunningham; 112. CP photo/Vancouver Sun-files; 113. CP photo/Paul Chiasson; 114. CP photo/Paul Chiasson; 117. CP photo/Russ Mant; 119. CP photo/Andrew Vaughan; 120. Paul Chiasson; CP photo/Fred Chartrand; Montreal Gazette/Dave Sidaway; 121. Paul Chiasson; 122. Montreal Gazette/Allen McInnis; AFP photo Roberto Schmidt; Wayne Cuddington/The Ottawa Citizen; 123. Chris Bolin/National Post; 124. AFP photo/Aaron Harris; 125. Julie Oliver/The Ottawa Citizen; 126. CP photo/Andre Forget; 127. Robert Galbraith/National Post 128. Robert Galbraith/National Post

Photo captions for preceding pages

Page 1 *November 8, 1993*
Page 2 *Just before the fourth and final ballot at the Liberal leadership convention in Ottawa, April 6, 1968*
Page 3 *At the Chateau Laurier hotel in Ottawa during the Liberal leadership convention, 1968*
Page 4 *With his Justice Minister Jean Chretien at constitutional talks in 1982*
Page 5 *Taking part in a classical Arabic dance with Saudi Arabian oil minister Sheikh Zaki Yamani, November 19, 1980*
Page 6 *Walking down the grandstand steps to present the Grey Cup trophy to the victorious Montreal Alouettes, November 28, 1970*
Page 9 *Walking to work on his 80th birthday*

Contents

Chronology

OCT. 18, 1919 Joseph Philippe Pierre Yves Elliott Trudeau is born in Montreal, the second child and first son of Jean-Charles Emile Trudeau and Grace Elliott Trudeau.

1933 Travels with family to Europe.

1934 Forms the Club of the Dying, requiring pranks for membership: "I developed a trick that involved going rigid and toppling forward, putting out my hands to break the fall only a split second before hitting the floor."

APRIL 10, 1935 Father dies, age 47, five days after he had contracted pneumonia: "His death truly felt like the death of the world. That's the only way I can put it."

1940 Receives BAH from Jean-de-Brebeuf College, Montreal.

1940–1943 Studies law at University of Montreal; develops a fondness for skiing.

1943 Graduates with honours.

1944 Travels to Mexico to learn Spanish but ditches official itinerary in favour of hitch-hiking across the country.

1944 Called to the Quebec bar.

1946 Graduates from Harvard with an MA in political economy.

1946–1948 Studies postgraduate law, economics and political science at Ecole libre des sciences politiques in Paris and the London School of Economics.

1948 Arrested and charged for espionage during travels through Middle East (also went to Europe and southern Asia), when mistaken for a spy because of his long beard and general appearance: He was dressed in traditional headdress and carried a walking stick and knapsack.

1949 Returns to Canada and allies himself with asbestos workers in Eastern Townships of Quebec; arrested by provincial police on April 22 and detained for a short time.

1949–51 Joins Privy Council Office in Ottawa as economic and policy advisor.

1950 Co-founds and edits the monthly left-of-centre political review magazine, *Cité Libre*.

1951 Quits Privy Council to travel to Africa, Asia, Europe and Moscow for a Communist international economic conference.

1952 Enters private law practice in Quebec, specializing in labour law and civil liberties.

1956 Paddles down the Mackenzie River in the Northwest Territories with Professor Frank R. Scott of McGill University; co-founds the political organization Le Rassemblement, "to defend and promote democracy in Quebec against the threats posed by corruption and authoritarianism; publishes *La greve de l'amiante* (*The Asbestos Strike*).

1958 Publishes "Some Obstacles to Democracy in Quebec" in the *Canadian Journal of Economics and Political Science*.

1960 Attempts to canoe from Florida to Cuba on April 30 with friends but high winds force them to abort crossing after 80 kilometres; Quebec Liberal party under Jean Lesage wins power on June 22, beginning the Quiet Revolution; Trudeau tours the People's Republic of China with delegation of Canadian intellectuals and labour activists Sept. 13 to Oct. 22.

1961 Publishes with Jacques Hebert *Two Innocents in Red China*, a witty account of the journey; Trudeau becomes associate professor at the University of Montreal, specializing in civil liberties and constitutional law, and works with the Institut de recherches en droit public.

1965 Publishes "Federalism, Nationalism, and Reason" in *The Future of Canadian Federalism*.

SEPT. 10, 1965 Convenes a press conference with Gerard Pelletier and Jean Marchand to announce their candidacy as Liberals for seats in the House of Commons.

NOV. 8, 1965 Wins election to the Commons from Quebec riding of Mount Royal.

JANUARY, 1966 Chosen to serve as Prime Minister Lester B. Pearson's parliamentary secretary.

1967 Serves as delegate to France-Canada Interparliamentary Association meetings in Paris; serves as Canadian delegate to the United Nations General Assembly.

APRIL 4, 1967 Sworn in as minister of justice and attorney-general of Canada.

DEC. 20, 1967 Introduces an omnibus bill of amendments to Criminal Code.

1967 Meets his future wife, Margaret Joan Sinclair, of North Vancouver, during a water-skiing holiday on the island of Moorea in Tahiti.

FEB. 16 1968 Declares candidacy for the leadership of the Liberal Party of Canada.

FEBRUARY–APRIL 1968 Sweeps nation with his own brand of charisma henceforth dubbed "Trudeaumania."

MARCH 1968 Publishes *Federalism and the French Canadians*, the English edition of his writings on nationalism.

APRIL 6, 1968 Elected leader of the Liberal party at convention in Ottawa.

APRIL 20, 1968 Becomes 15th prime minister of Canada when Pearson tenders his resignation.

JUNE 25, 1968 Leads the Liberals to overwhelming victory in federal election, winning 155 of 264 seats in the House of Commons.

1968 Described by media philosopher Marshall McLuhan as a "made-for-TV politician," the master of the sound bite long before media coaching became a prerequisite of office.

JUNE 9, 1969 Legislates Official Languages Act in Parliament, requiring English-French bilingualism in federal operations.

JANUARY, 1970 Escorts Barbra Streisand to National Arts Centre function in Ottawa.

OCTOBER, 1970 Invokes the War Measures Act, suspending protection of civil liberties during the October Crisis, when the separatist terrorist group Front de Liberation du Quebec (FLQ) kidnapped James Cross, British trade commissioner, and Quebec cabinet minister Pierre Laporte, who was later killed.

MARCH 4, 1971 Marries Margaret Joan Sinclair and honeymoons in British Columbia; groom is 51 and bride is 22.

DEC. 25, 1971 Becomes father for the first time, to Justin Pierre James Trudeau.

OCT. 30, 1972 Retains power of Liberals in federal election, though popularity is waning; governs with minority together with New Democratic Party.

1972 Appoints Muriel McQueen Fergusson first female Speaker of the Senate.

JAN. 16, 1973 Mother dies, age 82.

DEC. 25, 1973 Becomes father for a second time on Christmas Day, to Alexandre Emmanuel (Sacha).

MAY 8, 1974 Obtains vote of no-confidence in House of Commons from NDP with support of the opposition Progressive Conservatives.

JULY 8, 1974 Reinstated to parliamentary majority by voters in federal election, with the Liberals now controlling more than 140 seats in the House.

SEPT. 9, 1974 Wife Margaret Trudeau enters Royal Victoria Hospital in Montreal for treatment of psychiatric ailments and stays for two weeks.

OCT. 2, 1975 Third son, Michel Charles-Emile (Micha), is born.

JANUARY, 1976 Goes skin-diving with Fidel Castro on trip to Cuba with Margaret.

MAY 7, 1977 Performs pirouette behind Queen Elizabeth II's back at Buckingham Palace.

MAY 27, 1977 Separates from wife Margaret and retains custody of their three children.

1979 Described as "authoritarian, cold, and stingy" in Margaret Trudeau's exposé of her marriage, *Beyond Reason*.

MAY 22, 1979 Defeated by Joe Clark's Conservatives in federal election.

JUNE 4, 1979 Resigns as prime minister and becomes leader of opposition.

NOV. 21, 1979 Announces his retirement as leader of Liberal Party and retirement from public life.

DEC. 13, 1979 Decides to stay on and lead Liberals in the next election after government of Clark is defeated on a budgetary vote in House of Commons.

FEB. 18, 1980 Re-elected for a fifth term.

MARCH 3, 1980 Sworn in again as prime minister.

MAY 14, 1980 With less than a week to go in the Quebec referendum campaign, speaks at a rally of "No" to "sovereignty-association" with Canada; three in five Quebecers vote "No."

1980 Appoints Jeanne Sauve first female Speaker of the House of Commons.

APRIL 17, 1982 Patriates Canada's Constitution with Charter of Rights and Freedoms in ceremony with Queen Elizabeth II on Parliament Hill.

1984 Appoints Jeanne Sauve first female Governor-General.

FEB. 29, 1984 Announces decision to retire from politics.

APRIL 18, 1984 Former wife marries Fred Kemper, an Ottawa real-estate developer.

JUNE 16, 1984 Resigns officially as leader of the Liberal Party of Canada; succeeded by John Napier Turner; nominated for Nobel Peace Prize; awarded Albert Einstein International Peace Prize.

1984 Named a Companion of Honour of Britain.

SEPT. 20, 1984 Joins Montreal law firm Heenan Blaikie as senior counsel.

NOVEMBER, 1985 Named Companion of the Order of Canada.

MAY 27, 1987 Publishes open letter in Montreal and Toronto newspapers denouncing Brian Mulroney, the prime minister, and the premiers who negotiated the Meech Lake constitutional accord recognizing Quebec as a "distinct society."

AUG. 27, 1987 Criticizes the Accord before joint committee of the House of Commons and Senate.

MARCH 30, 1988 Speaks out against Meech Lake accord before the Senate.

MARCH 20, 1990 Publishes *Towards a Just Society*, a chronicle of the policy achievements of "the Trudeau years."

MAY 5, 1991 Becomes father to Sarah Elisabeth, with Deborah Coyne, a law professor and advisor on constitutional affairs to the government of Newfoundland and Labrador.

OCT. 30, 1995 Says he "sat on his hands" during Quebec referendum because No committee strategists indicated they did not want him involved; No side receives 50.5% victory

NOV. 13, 1998 Suffers death of youngest son, Michel, when an avalanche carries him into Kokanee Lake near Nelson, B.C.

JANUARY, 2000 Hospitalized for almost two weeks with serious bout of pneumonia.

JULY, 2000 Goes on vacation after having returned to work at Heenan Blaikie law firm.

SEPTEMBER, 2000 Said to be "not well" in statement made by sons Justin and Sacha.

SEPT. 28, 2000 Dies at his home in Montreal, age 80.

Roy MacGregor

Introduction

Something happened in Canada with the passing of Pierre Elliott Trudeau. In the midst of great loss, there had been a small discovery.

The passion was back.

No one knew how long it might last. Certain politicians hoped long enough, at least, to be of personal benefit; but other Canadians were far more intrigued by where it had come from than in where it might be going. The catalyst, obviously, had been the passing of Pierre Elliott Trudeau at the age of 80. The former prime minister had, as everyone in the country knew, been seriously ill for some time, so his death was hardly unexpected. But what caught the country off guard was the life force that flowed so freely about those events that marked his departure.

It was in the man who, at three o'clock in the morning, suddenly turned a perfect pirouette before the flag-draped coffin as the body of Pierre Trudeau lay in state on Parliament Hill. It was in the children, none of whom were even born when he was gone from office, who brought their single roses and crayoned cards to place by the Centennial Flame that was ignited the year he himself began sparking the country with new ideas. It was in the middle-aged, conservative-looking men and women who flashed discreet peace signs as his funeral cortège passed on the way to the train that would carry him to Montreal and the funeral that would officially mark the end of his time.

More than any scripted ceremony, however, it was the moment when that funeral train passed through the tiny Ontario town of Alexandria that will remain in memory. It was here, on a bright Monday morning, where an entire community— schoolchildren and veterans, mothers with children and farmers with other duties—

Mourners gather around the Centennial Flame on Parliament Hill, October 1, 2000, to pay their last respects.

suddenly decided to move as one and step so close to the tracks that they were able to slow the train down long enough to reach out and touch it as it passed, almost as if they felt a need to somehow *feel* his passing.

We all felt it, though hardly always in the same way. Some of what was written and said was overboard in both directions, for Pierre Trudeau was as disliked in parts of the country as he was admired in others. It would be both naïve and wrong to pretend he was as beloved in life as he seemed in death. His relationships with various parts of the country, Quebec included, suffered extraordinary mood swings: it was on the tarmac of the Calgary airport in 1968, for example, where the phenomenon known as "Trudeaumania" began—and it was in Calgary only a few years later, where he was most resented. Once the country threw him out of office; twice voters beyond Quebec turned their backs on him; he left before what would have been certain defeat. For every voice raised to credit him for the country another rose to blame him for the mess. In this, he was typically the politician.

Yet he was most assuredly not the typical politician. He was as talked about, and welcomed and cursed, as the weather. He was, whether some wish to admit it or not, much like his own country: expansive, diverse, exceptional, contradictory, charming, irritating, complex and, often, perplexing. He was, even by those who would never vote for him, as much a national mark as the most familiar Canadian landscapes, the one face and name in this country with resonance in other countries, with other people. It seemed, on reflection, that we mattered more when he was around.

His critics had both reason and right to point out the other side, but they rather missed the point of what was going on here. What was taking place was myth-making, and though he himself would protest, myth-making is always more a matter of passion than reason. The British have a sense of Churchill that does not always encompass his shortcomings. The Americans have a love for JFK that ignores his many flaws. Perhaps now, too, Canadians have a certain feel for a prime minister that refuses to be ensnared by policy interpretations and the historical register, for it is somehow larger than fact. Once a name evokes strong emotion, it enters a place in the public consciousness where nitpickers are rarely allowed.

Two years ago, Canadians began preparing for this moment when they watched Pierre Trudeau—seemingly for the first time in too many years—walk up the steps of Montreal's Saint-Viateur Roman Catholic Church on a dank, windswept day. It was the funeral to mark the passing of his 23-year-old son, Michel, lost to a British Columbia avalanche, and while so many wept with him that day for lost youth, it must now be acknowledged that many of the tears were for our own lost youth and presumed better times. The symbol of a generation's youth had become an old, broken man.

It was a most arresting phenomenon. A single man had become a calendar for the largest generation ever to pass through Canadian society. It was, like the music of the Beatles, a reminder of when everything seemed, for however short a time, possible. "He had captured," the historian Michael Bliss once wrote, "the spirit of the age." And now, more than three decades later, his death somehow *challenged* rather than captured that spirit again. Lost fires were briefly rekindled, and for a few warm fall days, anyway, personal tax breaks didn't seem like the single most pressing thing in the world to a great many people who believed they would not only change the world but get to know the world. Somewhere along the way, something important had been lost.

Perhaps that explains the hands of Alexandria, ordinary people reaching out to slow something that seemed to be moving too quickly.

Not just Pierre Trudeau's train, but their own precious time in Pierre Trudeau's country.

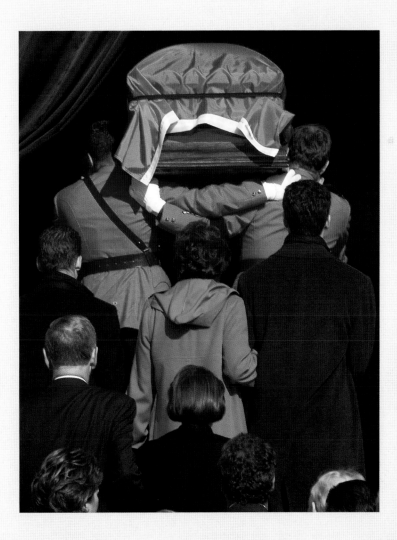

Left *A constant stream of mourners files past the flag-draped casket.*

Right *The casket of Pierre Trudeau is carried into the Parliment building, followed by his family and Jean Chretien and wife Aline for the first day of lying in state.*

Above *Cuban president Fidel Castro*

Left *Quebec premier Lucien Bouchard*

Above *Prime minister Jean Chretien and his wife Aline*

Above, right *Margaret Trudeau hugs her eleven-year-old daughter, Alicia Kemper.*

Right *Chretien embraces Justin while Margaret looks on.*

Above *Canadians wait in line long into the evening to pay their respects in Ottawa.*

Left *Sacha (foreground) and Justin*

Entries from books of condolences and from messages left with flowers in Ottawa on Parliament Hill and at Trudeau's Montreal home.

"Pierre Elliott Trudeau was so many things to so many people."

"To me, he was a visionary, a man of principles and a great person.
I and my generation owe our way of life to his thoughts.
There have been many words to describe him but the best words are,
'He was a great Canadian.'"

"Thanks to a wonderful Canadian for giving us the freedoms we
enjoy today. He will be greatly missed."

"What a great loss for Canada and mankind. Thanks for all you have done, from the Bercer family."

"He was a part of my youth and an inspiration to us all. He will be remembered for his repatriation
of the Constitution — always remembered."

"A true Canadian and patriot. You will be missed. My condolences to your family. You were many things
to many people but mostly you were a real Canadian."

"You were a good man. Peace be with you. We'll miss you."

Tributes

"In Canada, Pierre Elliott Trudeau is the sole figure who has continually dominated our imaginations and our spirits for nearly 40 years. His intelligence, often acerbic, always brilliant, exercised a formidable and irresistible fascination which intrigued us all. We were engaged, and frequently enthralled by this man who told us in his own words that 'in high school . . . I had already made up my mind to swim against the tide.'" Adrienne Clarkson, Governor-General of Canada

"He was, in simple human terms, a giant of a man. There is no question that when he [first] ran in the 1968 election campaign, he came to incarnate a sense of hope for the country, of what we could be. If he had a fault, it was that he thought all of the country had all of the talents that he did. That set probably too high a standard for most of Canada. But he was an extraordinary man." Joe Clark, the former Tory prime minister who defeated Mr. Trudeau's Liberals in the 1979 election, only to lose another election to him one year later

"Pierre Trudeau was the most remarkable Canadian of his generation. He had intellect, a vision . . . flair, and a great deal of personal courage." John Turner, former Liberal prime minister who served in Trudeau's Cabinet

"Although we had significant political disagreements at times, I have always readily acknowledged his great skill and determination in seeking to persuade Canadians of the value of his vision of Canada. History will eventually judge us all, but I have no doubt Mr. Trudeau will be remembered as a gallant political warrior who loved his country and devoted much of his life to its service." Brian Mulroney, former Conservative prime minister

"A generation of Canadians who came of age in the 1960s and 70s remembers Pierre Trudeau as the prime minister who defined that optimistic era. His belief in a bilingual, multilingual Canada and a strong social safety net helped to shape the values of Canadians." Alexa McDonough, NDP leader

"Pierre Trudeau was one of Canada's most colourful and passionate political figures of the 20th century, and his legacy will live on in Canadian history. Alberta had its differences with the former prime minister on some issues. But no one ever doubted his commitment to a strong, united Canada or to its principles of justice and equality. He fought hard for this country, and his contributions will not be forgotten." Ralph Klein, Alberta Premier

"Over the 20 years Mr. Trudeau spent in federal politics, and even beyond, he was a passionate defender of this nation, of our federal system and of the truly Canadian belief that our identity as Canadians is not compromised but strengthened when we identify ourselves in other ways. You can be a proud Quebecois, Trudeau said, and a proud Canadian. You can be a proud citizen of Saskatchewan, he said, and a proud and important citizen of this nation. He was an accomplished lawyer and scholar, a prolific writer—truly a man of many rare intellectual gifts." Roy Romanow, Saskatchewan Premier

"There's no politician that has left an impression on this country like he did. He inspired love, hatred, he interested a whole generation of young people in politics, he made politics a noble profession. People pretended to know him, but nobody really did, that was part of his mystique . . . he made us different in the world." David Peterson, former Liberal premier of Ontario

"Whether you agreed with Mr. Trudeau's vision or policies or not, he had a vision and he had ideas and you couldn't be indifferent. He changed the constitutional framework forever by the intro-duction of the Charter of Rights and Freedoms." Preston Manning, former Reform leader

"He was exceptionally gifted, absolutely brilliant and clearly unequivocal about his ideas. I believe that in the last 40 or 50 years, no one put Canada on the world map of international affairs as well as he did in a constructive and assertive fashion. I believe that his imprint on Canada will be long felt and remembered, particularly through the Charter of Rights and Freedoms. Equally important was his vision for a strong and just country, for which he fought hard." Ujjal Dosanjh, British Colombia Premier

"A redoubtable opponent, he always defended with conviction and tenacity the values which he sought to share." Gilles Duceppe, Bloc Quebecois Leader

"Mr. Trudeau wanted a Canada with a supreme federal government. I strove for a Canada with the provinces using their resources and distinctive strengths for a stronger whole. Yet through it all we never tried to deceive each other and we presented our different views directly and with candour." Peter Lougheed, former Alberta premier who waged a political war with Trudeau over the National Energy Program

"I'll always remember standing on St. George Street [in Toronto]. I had to meet my daughter and her mother phoned her and said Trudeau just died. In 1963, I was in Grade 5 in Orangeville and [my teacher] came in and a classmate said, 'Does this mean there's going to be a world war?' You knew you'd remember the moment of [John F.] Kennedy's death. And yeah, it'll be the same [here for Canadians]. He was an icon. I'm 47, but the first time that you really felt that Canada was a force on the world stage was when Trudeau was prime minister. You either loved him or you hated him, but he was provocative and he was evocative." Stephen LeDrew, president of Liberal Party of Canada

"[He was a prime minister] with vision, political courage and great personal style." Tony Blair, British Prime Minister

"I was sad when I heard the news because he had done so much for the country. He tried to make everyone equal and tried to make it work. When Trudeau was in power and running the country, I was a kid, I was 18 years old. My dad was a blue-collar guy and he always felt that Pierre Trudeau tried to take care of the whole country." Wayne Gretzky, former NHL hockey player who met Trudeau a few times, the last time during the 1984 Canada Cup tournament

"He was an extraordinary leader." Mike Harris, Ontario Premier

"He just had a very generous view of Canada; there aren't many voices any more that speak that way so it's a great big loss. [Working for him] was like working for the most exciting corporation in the world." Patrick Gossage, Trudeau's former press secretary

"He was our first contemporary charismatic telegenic politician. He was perhaps the last Canadian nationalist to be a politician and possibly what will distinguish his legislative career will be the Canadian Charter and Rights and Freedoms, but that is down the road for history to decide." Dalton Camp, long-time New Brunswick Conservative

"He was a giant compared to pygmies. My strongest political memory of him is standing up and facing the Quebec separatists in the eye in 1970 when they were throwing rocks and bottles at him. He had remarkable courage. I remember being on the floor of the Ottawa auditorium in 1968 and I saw Charles Lynch whisper in Trudeau's ear that Martin Luther King had just been assassinated. His face collapsed utterly in despair. It was a staggering moment." Mel Hurtig, Edmonton-based author and economic nationalist

"As prime minister for nearly a generation, Pierre Trudeau opened a dynamic new era in Canadian politics and helped establish Canada's unique imprint on the global stage." Bill Clinton, U.S. President

"He could sure throw you but he really listened to the question and he never gave you the predictable, easy answer. He was always two moves ahead of you. The arrogance was there, the certitude, the brilliance. It's so difficult watching the other politicians paying tribute to him when you realize there is simply no one cut from this cloth any more. You almost resent today's politicians trying to put themselves in his shoes." Peter Gzowski, author and broadcaster

"He started a revolution in social mores in this country . . . We had a number of clashes behind closed doors. I found him to be brilliant and thoughtful." Dave Barrett, former premier of British Columbia and former federal MP

"The government of the Northwest Territories joins the nation this evening in mourning the death of the Right Honourable Pierre Elliott Trudeau, one of Canada's great political leaders and statesmen . . . Mr. Trudeau loved the wilderness of Northern Canada. With his friends, he paddled our northern rivers and carried his bedroll across our arctic and subarctic terrain. He visited the North both as prime minister and after his retirement. To all Canadians he was an icon; to the North, he was a friend." Statement from the government of the Northwest Territories

"He was able to speak on the world stage as an equal to other world leaders, even if they were in fact much more powerful." Stephen Clarkson, Trudeau biographer

"I think he made a better Member of Parliament out of you because he forced you to be able to take positions and defend them. He had a great respect for the House of Commons. Although he pushed the members on the other side to their limit, he acted; when you came out and attacked him, he stood his ground and turned around and attacked back. He wasn't a passive man. He was a very passionate man." Gil Parent, House of Commons Speaker, who was first elected in 1974 and came in with the Trudeau sweep

"I feel orphaned. Canada has lost something today. Mr. Trudeau was Canada." Serge Joyal, Liberal Senator

Benares, India, January 1971

Justin Trudeau's Eulogy

"Friends, Romans, countrymen . . .

I was about six years old when I went on my first official trip. I was going with my father and my grandpa Sinclair up to the North Pole.

It was a very glamorous destination. But the best thing about it was that I was going to be spending lots of time with my dad because in Ottawa he just worked so hard.

One day, we were in Alert, Canada's northernmost point, a scientific military installation that seemed to consist entirely of low shed-like buildings and warehouses.

Let's be honest. I was six. There were no brothers around to play with and I was getting a little bored because dad still somehow had a lot of work to do.

I remember a frozen, windswept Arctic afternoon when I was bundled up into a Jeep and hustled out on a special top-secret mission. I figured I was finally going to be let in on the reason of this high-security Arctic base.

I was exactly right.

We drove slowly through and past the buildings, all of them very grey and windy. We rounded a corner and came upon a red one. We stopped. I got out of the Jeep and started to crunch across towards the front door. I was told, no, to the window.

So I clambered over the snowbank, was boosted up to the window, rubbed my

Even in the glare of publicity, father and son find time for a private moment.

Remembrance Day, Ottawa, 1981

sleeve against the frosty glass to see inside and as my eyes adjusted to the gloom, I saw a figure, hunched over one of many worktables that seemed very cluttered. He was wearing a red suit with that furry white trim.

And that's when I understood just how powerful and wonderful my father was.

Pierre Elliott Trudeau. The very words convey so many things to so many people. Statesman, intellectual, professor, adversary, outdoorsman, lawyer, journalist, author, prime minister. But more than anything, to me, he was dad.

And what a dad. He loved us with the passion and the devotion that encompassed his life. He taught us to believe in ourselves, to stand up for ourselves, to know ourselves and to accept responsibility for ourselves. We knew we were the luckiest kids in the world. And we had done nothing to actually deserve it. It was instead something that we would have to spend the rest of our lives to work very hard to live up to. He gave us a lot of tools. We were taught to take nothing for granted. He doted on us but didn't indulge. Many people say he didn't suffer fools gladly, but I'll have you know he had infinite patience with us. He encouraged us to push ourselves, to test limits, to challenge anyone and anything.

There were certain basic principles that could never be compromised. As I guess it is for most kids, in Grade 3, it was always a real treat to visit my dad at work. As on previous visits this particular occasion included a lunch at the parliamentary restaurant which always seemed to be terribly important and full of serious people that I didn't recognize. But at eight, I was becoming politically aware. And I recognized one whom I knew to be one of my father's chief rivals. Thinking of pleasing my father, I told a joke about him—a generic, silly little grade-school thing.

My father looked at me sternly with that look I would learn to know so well, and said: 'Justin, never attack the individual. One can be in total disagreement with someone without denigrating him as a consequence.'

Saying that, he stood up and took me by the hand and brought me over to introduce me to this man. He was a nice man who was eating with his daughter, a nice-looking blond girl a little younger than I was. My father's adversary spoke to me in a friendly manner and it was then that I understood that having different opinions from those of another person in no way precluded holding this person in the highest respect.

Because mere tolerance is not enough: we must have true and deep respect for every human being, regardless of his beliefs, his origins and his values. That is what my father demanded of his sons and that is what he demanded of our country. He demanded it out of love—love of his sons, love of his country. That is why we love him so. These letters, these flowers, the dignity of the crowds who came to say farewell—all of that is a way of thanking him for having loved us so much.

My father's fundamental belief never came from a textbook. It stemmed from his deep love for and faith in all Canadians and over the past few days, with every card, every rose, every tear, every wave and every pirouette, you returned his love.

It means the world to Sacha and me.

Thank you.

We have gathered from coast to coast to coast, from one ocean to another, united in our grief, to say goodbye. But this is not the end. He left politics in '84. But he came back for Meech. He came back for Charlottetown. He came back to remind us of who we are and what we're all capable of.

But he won't be coming back anymore. It's all up to us, all of us, now.

The woods are lovely, dark and deep. He has kept his promises and earned his sleep.

je t'aime papa.

Family Life

Left *Photo used for the 1976 Trudeau family Christmas card, taken at Harrington Lake. Left to right: Pierre, Michel, Justin, Margaret and Sacha*

Below, left *Trudeau carries Michel on his shoulders in Ottawa, May 11, 1979.*

Below, right *9-year-old Sacha and Trudeau paddling at the summer palace in Bang-Pa-In, Thailand, January 6, 1983*

Trudeau was well know for spending time with his sons. **Clockwise** *Being thrown in judo, running on the beach and posing for an informal holiday photograph*

Trudeau arrives with Justin at the Commonwealth Conference reception at Government House,

Ottawa, 1973.

Peter C. Newman

An Appraisal

Pierre Elliott Trudeau put us on the map. His acid candour, his intellectual acrobatics, his nose-thumbing at the staid traditions of this country's highest political office, qualified him as our first existential political hero: The man with the red rose in his buttonhole, who made us so proud that we elected him our prime minister for all but nine months of 16 turbulent years.

Now that he is gone, we must acknowledge that he saved Confederation by facing down the Front de Liberation du Quebec in 1970 and winning the referendum on French Canada's future a decade later. We mourn his passing because he made us aware that politics at its best consists not of backroom deals but of sharing the passions of our age.

Trudeau brought out the best and the worst in us, providing a feisty counterweight to his 19th-century predecessors. Trudeau was such an anomaly because within Official Ottawa, lucidity and frankness have always been in short supply, yet he was seldom willing to fudge seminal issues. His tossed-off quips and vulgarisms have left us a legacy of Trudeau aphorisms. In a 1968 TV interview, when asked about his prime ministerial duties: "I'm not going to let this job louse up my private life. And I won't wear sandals around 24 Sussex Drive. I'll go barefoot." In Winnipeg on Dec. 13, 1968, at a time of poor markets: "Well, why should I sell the Canadian farmers' wheat?" When asked in April, 1970, about Canada's policy on Biafra: "Biafra, Where's Biafra?"

That last quotation—used more frequently than any other to demonstrate Trudeau's arrogance, because Biafrans at the time were starving—illustrates how even the most offhand of his comments had a deeper meaning.

Unlike 99.9% of Canadians, Trudeau knew precisely where Biafra was, having not only visited that region of Nigeria during his world tour in the 1950s, but actually canoed down its principal river. Still, his government's policy was to recognize Nigeria, not Biafra, its breakaway province. Ever conscious that Quebec was pushing for separate international status, Trudeau was trying to underline his view that, legally, Biafra didn't exist, and that questions about it were comparable to asking him about "Laurentia"—the name French-Canadian nationalists gave their dream of an independent state.

Looking back on this remarkable prime minister and his times, it seems clear that we burdened him with expectations no mortal could meet. There was bound to be a gap between his deeds and intentions, between his promise and performance. But that didn't explain why he became such a lightning rod for our complaints and frustrations. I remember, near the end of his reign, watching with fascination a burly trucker at a motel near Red Deer who had lost his 45 cents in a vending machine. He stood back and kicked the thing. Nothing happened. He shook it nearly off its hinges. No luck. Then he took a deep breath, glared at the offending contraption and cursed: "God damn Trudeau anyway!"—and walked away.

Although Pierre Trudeau appeared to come out of nowhere, when he unexpectedly won the Liberal party leadership in 1968, he was, in fact, the product of a crammed and precisely plotted education that included stints at Harvard, the Sorbonne, the London School of Economics and the University of Montreal. His academic immersion lasted until he entered active politics at the advanced age of 46.

His father was a farmer's son who earned a law degree and established a chain of gasoline stations on Montreal Island, which he sold to Imperial Oil in 1932 for $1.4-million. The funds were reinvested so wisely that Pierre (born on Oct. 18, 1919), as well as his brother and sister, each became multi-millionaires. His father taught him order and discipline, while his mother, the former Grace Elliott, imbued him with a longing for personal freedom and the appreciation of intellectual pursuits.

Attending Montreal's Jean-de-Brebeuf College, run by the Jesuit teaching order, he absorbed the mysteries of Catholic doctrine, and first explored his ability to debate. It was there, too, that he began to excel at individual sports—high-diving, judo, skiing, gymnastics and canoeing. Then followed years of study at the University

"He was bold, charismatic and a visionary. He was everything a politician should be, but almost always isn't."

of Montreal (he was called to the Quebec Bar in 1943); at Harvard ("I realized we were being taught law as a trade in Quebec, not as a discipline. The majors in political science at Harvard had read more about Roman law and Montesquieu than I as a lawyer"); at the Ecoles Sciences Politiques at the Sorbonne in Paris; and at the London School of Economics, where he came under the influence of left-wing philosopher Harold Laski.

1938

In the two years that followed his formal education, Trudeau travelled the world in a solitary quest to taste new cultures and languages. The exact chronology of that time is unclear but his known ports of call included Belgrade, Vienna, Rome, Milan, Budapest, Istanbul, Warsaw, much of the Middle East, India and Pakistan. He was also expelled from Yugoslavia as an Israeli spy and penetrated Palestine aboard a truck of renegade Arabs, just before Partition in 1948. He later toured "Red" China; was picked up by the U.S. Coast Guard off Key West, Fla., trying to reach Fidel Castro's Cuba in a small boat; and caused a minor riot in Moscow's Red Square when he started to heave snowballs at the then-hallowed statue of Joseph Stalin. He was let off with a warning when he explained to a puzzled policeman that whenever he went to Ottawa he threw snowballs at the statue of Sir Wilfrid Laurier.

Trudeau returned to Canada in 1949 and, finding that Cardinal Leger had vetoed his application to teach political theory at the church-controlled University of Montreal, joined the Privy Council Office in Ottawa, under Liberal Prime Minister Louis St. Laurent.

The next three years made a deep impression on the young cosmopolitan: even though the prime minister of the day was a Quebecer, most French Canadians who worked for the federal government occupied only token positions. The French

language was used mainly by elevator operators and the maitre d' at Madame Burger's Restaurant in Hull, Quebec.

During the 1950s, Trudeau founded the intellectual review *Cité Libre*, which became an important catalyst in rallying intellectual dissent against the increasingly oppressive regime of Quebec Premier Maurice Duplessis. He also helped establish a pseudo-political movement named Le Rassemblement (which was dedicated to uniting opposition to the corrupt Union Nationale) and supported the Liberals in the 1960 election. A reform-minded Jean Lesage was brought into power. In a prophetic essay written at the time, Trudeau commented: "If, in the last analysis, we continually identify Catholicism with conservatism, and patriotism with immobility, we will lose by default that which is at play between all of our cultures."

The Trudeau of this period developed a reputation for skipping from cause to cause, idea to idea. His friend and fellow Quebecer, Jean Marchand, then the province's most militant union leader, recalled that, "Pierre took a long time to get involved in things. In any social or political adventure he had to overcome a considerable reluctance. As soon as he felt he was menaced with involvement, he left for the South of France." Despite his long absences, Trudeau did start to build a following among young teachers and lawyers in the province and managed to publish several books and 50 articles, including an epochal appeal for realism in Canadian politics, published simultaneously in *Cité Libre* and *The Canadian Forum*.

I remember calling on Trudeau at the time. He worked in a bare cubicle at the University of Montreal's Institute for Public Law, wearing outrageously ill-matched clothes. He told me that separatism in Quebec would never triumph because it could not transform itself into a broadly based popular movement.

Instead, it had become what Trudeau called "a bourgeois revolution—the uprising of people who were afraid they wouldn't have enough important jobs in the society of tomorrow. They thought that only an independent Quebec would solve their problems, because they would be its new elite and wouldn't have to share power and jobs with outsiders."

During the 1965 election campaign, when Trudeau, journalist Gerard Pelletier and Marchand became Liberal candidates, it was considered a great coup for Prime Minister Lester Pearson. At a time when support of the federal interest was an unpopular posture in their own milieu, these gallant, middle-aged revolutionaries took a risky stand, clearly identifying themselves as Quebecers who believed in the Canadian future. This was no easy decision for a trio whose professional lives had been devoted to fostering the social upheaval that became Quebec's Quiet Revolution. By joining Ottawa and the federal Liberals, they were rejecting the notion that the government of Quebec should be the solitary custodian of Canada's French fact.

Once in Ottawa, Trudeau found, as he had during his previous sojourn, that the ingrained attitude was to give only the trappings and seldom the substance of power to Quebec politicians and civil servants. Of the three dozen or so top-level bureaucrats who formed Ottawa's "Establishment," only one deputy minister—undersecretary of state for external affairs Marcel Cadieux—was a French Canadian. In the 11 most important government departments, only six of the 163 civil servants who received $14,000 a year or more were from Quebec. The entry into active federal politics of the trio of articulate reformers transformed the attitudes that produced such an obvious imbalance. The "three wise men" as they were called, were determined to claim the substance and not merely the illusion of federal power. Within months of arriving in Ottawa, Trudeau was named parliamentary assistant to the Prime Minister and appointed to several important committees. He represented Canada at the 21st session of the United Nations General Assembly in New York, and headed a task force on the possibility of changing Canada's constitution. He grew personally close to Lester Pearson, who recognized in Trudeau a man very different from the florid French Canadians who had preceded him. Despite Trudeau's eccentricities of dress, he possessed the qualities Pearson admired. He was the product of a rich and cultivated home, he had been educated abroad, had

"Trudeau was a leader, an honest man and he stood for what he said. I think of Trudeau as a symbol for everyone—a man of strong principles."

Above *With Prime Minister Pearson at the opening session of the Constitutional Conference in Ottawa, February 5, 1968*
Left *The Pearson cabinet; Trudeau is standing on the left*

travelled widely, was an avowed intellectual, a sometime reformer and a convinced internationalist.

On April 4, 1967—less than two years after he entered politics—Trudeau was appointed Minister of Justice and Attorney General of Canada, and set about trying to reform a badly outdated justice system.

During an interview I had with him at the time, he went directly to the core of his political philosophy: "This ministry," he declared, "should be regarded more and more as a department planning for the society of tomorrow, not merely acting as the government's legal advisor. It should combine the function of drafting new legislation with the disciplines of sociology and economics, so that it can provide a framework for our evolving way of life. We have to move the framework of society slightly ahead of the times."

From left to right: Pierre Trudeau, John Turner, Jean Chretien and Lester Pearson, 1976

Eight months later, he presented a reform package to the Commons and, while defending his ideas on CBC television, pronounced the magic phrase: "I want to separate sin from crime. You may have to ask forgiveness for your sins from God, but not from the Minister of Justice. There's no place for the state in the bedrooms of the nation." This was hardly a startling proposition, but it made a disproportionate impact on a society numbed by generations of politicians blowing through their moustaches about the gross national product, trade surpluses and equalization payments. It was the first intimation that Trudeau might be able to excite public opinion.

A small but resolute band of progressive Quebec Liberals tried to get Jean Marchand to run for leadership of the Liberal party, but when he decided that neither his command of English nor his health were up to the top job, Trudeau became the centre of their attention. If Pierre Trudeau's subsequent conquest of the Liberal party appears to have been predestined, with the other contenders for the leadership serving as mere flag-bearers, in the bleak chill of December, 1967, just before Pearson's resignation announcement, Trudeau's victory seemed more far fetched than inevitable.

Trudeaumania

Rideau Club denizens were fond of telling each other the story about the time he turned up on a Saturday morning at the Privy Council Office dressed in desert boots and a boiler suit. The commissionaire on duty, convinced he was a plumber who had his work sheet jumbled, turned him away at the door. When his name was mentioned casually in the early speculative talk about candidates, it was dismissed as a joke. ("How could anybody who combs his hair like that be Prime Minister of Canada?") In this uncertain preliminary stage, the contest for succession was little more than sentiment in search of a leader. Many Liberals felt they wanted a dramatic change from the Pearson brand of politics, a candidate who could re-establish public trust in the party and reawaken confidence in itself. But it was difficult to identify this urge with any of the obvious contenders so eagerly offering themselves for the job. Most of them—Paul Hellyer, Mitchell Sharp, Paul Martin, Robert Winters, Allan MacEachen, Joe Greene—seemed to represent the old instead of the new politics. Of the others, John Turner wasn't ready, and Eric Kierans' power base owed more to decency than delegate strength.

As soon as Trudeau hinted that he might be available, English Canadians, MPs, historians, communicators and progressive thinkers of every stripe began coalescing behind his candidacy. In a courting mood, but not committing himself, Trudeau left for a holiday in the South Pacific. "Before I make my decision," he told me before leaving, "I've got to find out whether it's really possible to do anything once I get into the Prime Minister's Office."

Following Trudeau's triumphant tour of the country selling a new constitutional reform package, and after his star performance at a federal-provincial conference (where he bested Quebec Premier Daniel Johnson), his candidacy became an accepted fact.

On Feb. 14, 1968, he announced it at a press conference, leaving little doubt that he would be a very different candidate from those who had gone before.

His popularity soared; even his fellow contenders didn't dare attack him. Riding a chartered jet and wearing his leather coat, Trudeau travelled 20,000 miles, making 30 stops, during his leadership campaign. Every appearance ignited standing ovations. He was able to establish personal contact with his audiences without strain, operating on a private wavelength the other candidates couldn't jam.

"A giant of wisdom and vision. A great fighter for justice and peace. A believer of his own principles, which elevate the state of every Canadian. Above all, a great human being. We mourn forever our loss."

A motel pool in Oakville, Ontario, during a campaign break, June 14, 1969

His emotional impact had been demonstrated most forcefully when he arrived for the convention by train: tsunamis of young girls (teenyboppers, as they were then called) welcomed him by throwing wedding rice, waving Valentines and squeaking in delight, gasping at the sight of him.

"Something happens to people's faces when they see Trudeau," Ron Haggart reported in *The Toronto Star.* "You can manufacture noise and screaming kids, but you cannot manufacture that excitement in the eyes of excited matrons and lawyers. It's not madness. It is belief."

The election that followed was a combination of coronation and Beatles tour. The teenyboppers with manes of streaming hair gripped their machine-autographed photos of Pierre-baby to their chests and shrieked whenever he deigned to kiss one of their swarming number. Bemused toddlers borne on their parents' shoulders were admonished to "remember him," as excitement surged across the country.

Press cameras whirred like hungry insects every time Trudeau stepped out of his prime ministerial jet, Caesar haircut intact, to make his triumphant way from one shopping centre plaza to the next.

Voters came prepared to be scandalized by a wild man in sandals spouting socialist slogans. Instead they found an immaculate, demure professor delivering proposals that sounded exciting but were hardly radical. Unable to classify him as a man of either the political right or the political left, most of Trudeau's listeners seemed happy to regard him simply as a man of the future. Awarded a conclusive majority (155 of 264 seats), Trudeau set out to govern a country that had, in effect, given him a blank cheque.

Trudeau's decade-and-half in office revolutionized Canadian society. He was determined to shake things up, and he did. He was at his best among small groups of insiders, and at his worst in the House of Commons.

He could rise to individual occasions (such as leader's days or soliloquies on foreign affairs) but most of the time he regarded Parliament as a boring necessity. He would turn aside Opposition queries with quips, non-sequiturs, historical allusions and the occasional "fuddle-duddle" expletive. He could be deadly with sloppy questioners. But more often he slouched through the sittings, following Orders of the Day with about as much interest as a bookie hearing last week's race results.

During his tenure he reduced Canada's Armed Forces to joke proportions, listing national defence as his Cabinet's 14th priority, just after price support for hogs. What Trudeau

President Jimmy Carter with Trudeau in the Oval Office at the White House, March 3, 1979

forgot was that, in the disarmament sweepstakes, your clout is equivalent to what you throw into the pot. Since Canada became the only nation in history to disarm unilaterally, Trudeau ended up zooming around the world to little avail, finding no takers for his grand peace initiatives. Everyone supported his cause but no one joined it.

His dealings with Washington were equally ineffective, though in the summer of 1982, he adroitly encapsulated American-Canadian relations when he told a scholarly audience: "Our main exports to the United States are hockey players and cold fronts. Our main imports are baseball players and acid rain."

Around the Cabinet table, Trudeau's ministers were reduced to a league of awed men and women, not so much afraid to challenge his views as uncertain of their own in the face of his strength. Most of the time, Trudeau and his entourage acted as if they believed the country could be divided into three self-contained protectorates: Lower Canada (Quebec), Upper Canada (Ontario) and Outer Canada

(Everything Else). Trudeau catered to Lower Canada, ruled Upper Canada and ignored Outer Canada.

As prime minister, Trudeau largely ignored the 12 million Canadians west of Toronto's Humber River. Canadians unfortunate enough to live closer to the sunset, had to be satisfied with the gesture that came to symbolize his attitude toward the region: giving the finger to the citizens of Salmon Arm, B.C. His government staged grandiloquent gabfests such as the Western Economic Opportunities Conference in July, 1973, that promised much and accomplished nothing.

What Trudeau never understood was that the pervasive impact of television and personal travel had endowed Western Canadians with the same aspirations and ambitions as those that motivated the lives of the sophisticated dudes in the urban East. (If he thought about British Columbia at all, it was as a troublesome outpost on a distant second shore. Harry J. Boyle, the witty chairman of the CRTC, recognized the syndrome, aptly describing the Trudeau mandarins as "always running around scared that somebody was going to dump tea into Victoria Harbour.")

No matter what was happening in the West the country's intelligentsia, with Trudeau in the vanguard, was fixated on Quebec as the focus of change and action. "Language rights" was the instrument Trudeau used to open up the rest of the country to Quebec. He hammered through an Official Languages Act that permitted Quebecers to speak French with federal officials across the country and appointed francophones to every major economic portfolio, including Finance, proving conclusively that they were no worse than their anglophone counterparts.

This orderly process was interrupted in October, 1970, when two armed revolutionaries kidnapped British trade commissioner James Cross from his Montreal home. These and other acts of terror, particularly the brutal murder of Quebec labour minister Pierre Laporte, prompted Trudeau to call out the Armed Forces and invoke the War Measures Act, which Canada had never before applied in peacetime. Its provisions, which allowed police to search and arrest suspects without warrants, jail them without charge and hold them without bail, seemed to go against everything Trudeau believed as a lifelong advocate of basic human rights.

"It's more important to maintain law and order," he decreed, "than to worry about those whose knees tremble at the sight of the army." When CTV reporter Tim

Trudeau switched from his regular car to the National Defence department's armored Cadillac in the wake of

terrorist activity by the FLQ in Montreal and the kidnapping of British diplomat James Cross, October 5, 1970.

Queen Elizabeth II signs Canada's constitutional proclamation in Ottawa on April 17, 1982.

Ralfe asked how far he would go in support of law and order, Trudeau delivered his most famous challenge: "Just watch me!" Indeed, the nation watched transfixed as more than 450 suspected activists were arrested, including 150 alleged members of the FLQ, without warrants or bail.

The emergency passed, leaving an unhealed wound, but it had serious political consequences. Trudeau's macho reaction to Quebec nationalism helped fan separatism in the province, allowing Rene Levesque's Parti Quebecois to triumph over the corrupt Bourassa regime six years later. Levesque eventually escalated his cause into a referendum, held in the spring of 1980. It turned out to be Trudeau's finest hour. His powerful speeches and carefully timed appearances diffused the sovereignty issue, allowing him to enlist the rest of the country in his grand strategy of pushing through his constitutional reforms. When the federal side decisively won the referendum, Trudeau turned his attention to fashioning a new Constitution, because it would allow him to enshrine language rights, sever Canada's umbilical cord with Mother Britain, and turn into law his cherished Charter of Rights and Freedoms.

"You were more appreciated abroad than you were in this country."

That Charter has permanently transformed the relationship of Canadians to their governments, allowing the courts to strike down laws that breach guarantees of freedom of speech, religion and association. "The Charter," proclaimed Chief Justice Antonio Lamer, "represents a revolution on the scale of the introduction of the metric system, the great medical discoveries of Louis Pasteur, and the invention of penicillin and the laser." The tested tradition of parliamentary supremacy was replaced by judicial dominance, turning judges into active players within the political process. The most harmful aspect of his legacy was to entrench a "notwithstanding" clause, which allows dissenting premiers to override the Charter at will. It was, for example, invoked by Robert Bourassa to implement the 1988 language bill prohibiting outdoor signs other than in French, in defiance of the Charter's guaranteed freedom of expression. Trudeau later publicly admitted that the Charter was "fundamentally flawed because of the override clause." Through a series of intricate manoeuvres, Trudeau obtained the blessing of every province except Quebec and, on April 17, 1982, the Queen signed the proclamation that gave Canada a homegrown Constitution at last.

In the winter of 1984, Pierre Trudeau decided to quit because he couldn't think

of a good reason to stay. The Constitution was home; bilingualism was in place; his peace initiatives were stalled; the economy seemed beyond salvation. There was no fun in the nation's business any more. "I was my own best successor, but I decided not to succeed myself," he mused, in character to the end.

The initial reaction was unexpectedly muted. Some confirmed Trudeau haters like the Toronto *Sun*'s Peter Worthington, declared that he wanted "to drive a wooden stake through Trudeau's heart," to make sure he was really finished. Most commentators, however, agreed with Trudeau's blood enemy, Rene Levesque, who remarked: "He sure made things more interesting—not necessarily more appealing, but certainly more interesting."

That was true enough. Pierre Trudeau was the most activist prime minister this country has ever elected. The reason most Canadians were so ambivalent about the man was that they remained ambivalent about their country.

We were glad to have had him as a visitor in our time—and glad he was moving on. Except that he didn't.

During the decade following his departure, Trudeau remained a powerful absence. Though he was out of office, he was never out of contact. He consulted daily with such trusted former lieutenants as Tom Axworthy, Gordon Gibson, Dick O'Hagan and the always cheerful Keith Davey. Probably his most frequent caller was the former deputy prime minister Senator Allan MacEachen, who regularly brought parliamentary business to a halt by rallying the 73 senators (nearly all appointed by Trudeau) to vote against the Mulroney administration. The Red Chamber became Trudeau's government-in-exile, where his Liberal warlocks obstructed pivotal Tory legislation including free trade with the United States, the goods and services tax, and the drug patent bill.

Apart from the activist Senate perpetuating Trudeau's legacy, there was a good case to be made that during the Mulroney years, Trudeau exercised control over the Conservative government's priorities. Nearly every fiscal initiative Mulroney tried to launch was constrained by Trudeau's legacy. During his 16 years in power, Trudeau had turned the balanced national accounts he inherited into a $38.5-billion deficit and increased the national debt by 1,200%, from $17-billion to more than $200-billion. By the time Mulroney took over, less than 15% of the annual

Facing page *Many of Trudeau's famous impromptu moments were revealed later to have been fully rehearsed. Here, he balances a golf club on his chin before a laughing Jean Marchand.*

budget was made up of discretionary spending, so that the Boyo from Baie Comeau was robbed of any wiggle room to pay for the many promises he had made.

His pivotal contributions to the defeat of Brian Mulroney's major constitutional initiatives—the Meech Lake and Charlottetown accords—rekindled Trudeau's popularity, and allowed him to get off some great one-liners. Attacked for being a man of the past, he shrugged and replied: "I suppose Pythagoras was yesterday's man also, but two and two still makes four." As always, he was impartial, criticizing Jean Chretien ("he knows his limitations") with the same throwaway arrogance that he applied to Joe Clark ("headwaiter of the provinces") and Brian Mulroney ("a sniveller, a constitutional pyromaniac").

Only now that he is no longer with us, can we fully measure Trudeau's worth. His passing awakens the profound feeling that we somehow let him down. His intelligence and charisma turned his stewardship into a shining political season. It demanded a sophisticated public response that Canadians never found comfortable. His death robs us of the chance to balance that equation.

Still, Pierre Elliott Trudeau was by long odds the most resolute leader this country ever had. His shimmering intellect cast all other pretenders in the shade. He broadened our universe by making the world his stage. Above all, no matter what he did, in office or out, he always exercised his ultimate civil liberty: the right to be himself.

Trudeau drives away from Government House, June 4, 1979, in his Mercedes sports car after resigning as prime minister.

Said with Style

The pithy lines of several former prime ministers are seared into Canadians' memories, but none are as well known or as barbed as those of Pierre Trudeau, nor said with such style....

1991

"...I am a pragmatist, I try to find the solution for the present situation, and I do not feel myself bound by any doctrines or any rigid approaches to any of these problems." Speech to the Canadian Club, May 23, 1968

1975

"The philosophy of the Liberal Party is very simple—say anything, think anything, or better still, do not think at all, but put us in power because it is we who can govern you best." 1963

1990

**"Well, why should I
sell the Canadian
farmers' wheat?"**
At Liberal Party meeting,
December 13, 1968

**"Vive la France, et vive les Anglais, aussi.
Et vive la republique des patates frites."** Replying to a
heckler during 1968 election campaign, who shouted
"Vive la France!"

1968

57

1973

"Meet my girlfriend." Introducing his new wife, Margaret Sinclair, 22, to a crowd in Ottawa four days after their marriage in March, 1971

1983

1984

"Bleeding hearts." His description of those who objected to the mass arrests under the War Measures Act during the October Crisis of 1970

"Each man has his own reasons, I suppose, as driving forces, but mine were twofold. One was to make sure that Quebec wouldn't leave Canada through separation, and the other was to make sure that Canada wouldn't shove Quebec out through narrowmindedness." Television interview, 1973

1983

"I was my best successor but I decided not to succeed myself."

In announcing his retirement, February, 1984

**"That bunch of snivellers should
simply have been sent packing
and been told to stop having
tantrums like spoiled
adolescents."** On Quebec's
demands in the Meech
Lake Accord, 1987

1968

Alanna Shepherd watches the funeral train passing through Alexandria, Ontario.

Roy MacGregor

Train Number 638

I have no idea who he was. A farmer on the east side of the tracks just before Cassel-man, an older man in coveralls and high rubber boots who stood dead centre in his field as surely as if he had surveyed and paced out the precise spot to stand for effect. An old farmer at attention, his right hand raised in salute.

They talk about the crowds that came out to watch special train No. 638 pass through these small eastern Ontario and western Quebec communities on its way from Ottawa to Montreal, and so they should, but there was something about the loners that would have appealed mightily to the loner who lay in the rear of this sad train, the Canadian flag that draped Pierre Trudeau's coffin barely visible to those who came to clap and wave and, in more than a few cases, salute.

Loners like the farmer in his field. The man who seemed to squeeze out of the thick bush running down toward Alexandria. The woman who stood at the side of a bank heading into Coteau, first station on the Quebec side, a baby on her back smiling at the train while she sobbed.

All of them felt the same compelling kinship with this late prime minister who saw himself as the solitary paddler, who was seen by us as the solitary gunfighter, and who remained oddly distant even to the two loving sons who stood to each side of the vestibule between the family car and the domed coffin car, and stared down in amazement into more red and streaming eyes than would seem reasonable for an 80-year-old man 16 years out of office.

But if reason was his guide, passion would be theirs. In a quiet way that is only now becoming apparent, the people of Canada kept Pierre Trudeau in a special office that had nothing to do with election and everything to do with feeling.

No. 638 carrying Trudeau's casket through the town of Alexandria.

It was not that there was any natural empathy between the man dead and, say, the man standing dead centre in his corn field. This, after all, was Pierre Elliott Trudeau, who once asked farmers, "Why should I sell your wheat?" who once, in a telling moment, pressed his face to a limousine window carrying him through a southwestern Ontario night, stared out at the flickering farm lights and wondered aloud to an aide, "Whatever do they do?"

A millionaire very much to the manor born, an intellectual and an ascetic—and yet, as No. 638 began passing through Alexandria, people who had never met him, some of them not even born when he was gone from office, moved closer and closer to the train until they could reach out and touch it and actually feel his passing.

It caused the engineers nervousness, but it sent chills up the backs of those inside the train staring out in far more wonder than those staring in.

By this point, there were tears on both sides of the glass.

It is almost impossible to describe the effect of staring out at the country and seeing a face that you had not seen for far too long.

The first surprise was barely out of the Ottawa station, the funeral train picking up speed as it passed along the back of the Ottawa-Carleton Transpo shops, and seeing that the mechanics had all laid down tools for the moment and come to the back fence, where they stood with big, rough hands folded as if they were in the midst of a recital.

At Casselman it was the volunteer fire brigade, in uniform, at attention. On the other side of the tracks, an atom hockey team in their new sweaters. Another mile or so, golfers standing up from their putts because, for once, they sought distraction.

It was the railway worker at the side of the tracks, his yellow plastic coveralls smeared in grease but his hardhat cradled at his side as he held attention. It was the farmer on the tractor at the gravel crossing, his cap off in respect. It was the construction workers who had crawled out of the hole they were digging, the front-end loader behind them raised and stilled in its own salute.

It was the woman holding up the cherry paddle with the rainbow-coloured voyageur scarf wrapped around it. The man with the flag attached to a hockey stick he was waving. The cars that raced alongside the tracks, maple leaf flags snapping in the wind.

But more than anything it was the hands of Alexandria. Inside, you could hear them squeak along the metal. You could see the people stepping forward—too close, it seemed—and reaching out as if it seemed exactly the right thing to do, and most assuredly it was.

The train moved so slowly through the crowd—"an especially dignified pace," an official had called it—and a piper could be heard playing "The Last Post." The train passed a group of uniformed Legionaires, all at attention, all saluting, and then, immediately after, a corps of young cadets, all at attention, all saluting, and if the lines in their faces made the two groups seem decades apart, their line of sight made them all the same: Canadians showing their enormous respect.

A few moments down the line, where a school was turned out, the extraordinary power of Pierre Elliott Trudeau's presence, in death as well as life, was on display: Kids were taking off their baseball caps.

Some may say it was the weather that brought so many out, that some strange weather pattern was bringing the summer that forgot Canada back for this special moment. Perhaps so, but much more than the weather seemed in retreat for the moment. The way they held on to their flags, the messages in their scribbled signs, all made the day feel more out of 1967 than 2000. There was a feeling in the air that has not been around for some time; and just like the weather, no one could tell how long it might last.

A Dominion Day visit to Kelowna, British Columbia, July 2, 1971. Trudeau flew from Ottawa to help celebrate British Columbia's Centennial and revealed another talent—unicycle riding.

No. 638 slowed for the towns and the villages but, to make up for lost schedule, it sped up through the bush and the fields and the swamp. It might have slowed here, too, for the loner in back was passing, for the final time, through the country he loved best.

The leaves are turning late—poplar only now yellowing, maple with but a hint of what is to come—but the sumac red as blood for a man who once wrote that long train rides will only exhaust you, but "paddle a hundred miles in a canoe and you are already a child of nature."

Not far from Maxville, a great blue heron lifted off from a marsh, its graceful wings tipping as it turned and was gone from sight. Along the Quebec-Ontario border, thousands of Canada geese suddenly spooked from the whistle and rose as one, nearly darkening the eastern sky. He would have liked that. He would have liked the way the October light played across the fields and the slow wash of the Nation River on such a windless day. Always quick with the perfect quote, he might himself have turned to Wordsworth to explain the weather: "Nature never did betray/ The heart that loved her."

It was a short train, two locomotives, three cars—one for the media, one buffer car carrying the protocol officers, the RCMP pallbearers and the funeral organizers, one for the family and friends such as former Trudeau minister Marc Lalonde and Senator Jacques Hebert and former governor-general Romeo LeBlanc—and then the special car carrying the coffin, a small RCMP honour guard and those who had to ensure the coffin rode properly.

"We are bringing Mr. Trudeau home," Lalonde said when he and Hebert briefly came up to sit and talk in the media car.

It was a perfect quote and an admirable gesture, and for a while the cameras and microphones surrounded them and prodded for more telling words, but gradually it all broke up and the two old friends went back to the family car and the cameras turned again to the windows.

The real story, the telling one, was outside. No quotes, no names. Yet never so eloquent, never so easily identified as Canadians.

Justin and Sacha Trudeau, seemingly amazed at first by the response, began reaching out as they slowed for the crowds. They took flowers. They

"Dear Justin and Sacha: I would like to wish you our condolences on your great loss. We feel the pain, too, for Canada's father is no more. He invited us to this country when I was only nine, and now this land is my home. I would like to take a moment and thank him for all that he gave us."

Justin (left) and Sacha Trudeau lean out of the funeral train.

touched hands. They, more than anyone else, felt exactly what was going on here.

The train passed through the fields and villages and on between the factories and warehouses of the outer city and still there were faces and flags filling every window. They stood on the platforms and stood on the pedestrian crossovers and waved from backyards and bedroom windows.

One man, another understanding loner, stood in the middle of a construction site on a mound of clay. His shoes were polished black. His suit was pressed. His shirt newly ironed. And his tie so tight it seemed he must have been choking back even before 638 came into sight.

They took him again by car up through the streets of Montreal. As Lalonde had said, where he was born and raised, and where he returned to once he retired. As another Montrealer once said of this special city, "my time, his place." In this case, our time, too, if no one minds.

They stopped at City Hall where he once again lay in state and the same eerie silence that was last felt on Parliament Hill now settled at the steps of Montreal's Hotel de Ville. Thousands of people, hundreds of flags, not a single voice.

At least not until they began carrying him up the steps, the flag and the coffin rising on the shoulders of the eight uniformed Mounties.

And then one man's voice, one man began singing "O Canada."

Gradually, other voices joined in until, as the coffin rose higher and higher, so too did the voices carrying the national anthem.

Someone let go a balloon in the shape of a red rose, and it circled and circled over the heads of the people as if momentarily unsure which direction to take.

A lone balloon, symbolizing one very special life and, perhaps for the moment, all those who came out over several days to be alone with their thoughts.

Pierre Trudeau was home.

Public Life

Liberal MPs vote on the question of repatriating the Constitution in the House of Commons, December 2, 1981.

Trudeau makes his views known to the Senate committee studying the Meech Lake constitutional accord, 1988.

Above *With Indira Ghandi in New Delhi,*
November 29, 1983
Left *Walking with officials in China,*
1973 (Deng Xia Ping is second from left).
Margaret is in the background.

*Always happy to show his physical adroitness, Trudeau jumps on a trampoline in 1974, **above left**, gets ready to dive in Guyana in 1974, **above**, and performs hands-only pushups during a break from a boat trip down the Yukon's Nahanni River in 1970, **below left**.*

Above *The famous pirouette behind Queen Elizabeth during a picture session at Buckingham Palace, May 7, 1977.* **Above right** *Another pirouette in Ottawa after the proclamation of the Constitution Act, April 18, 1982.* **Below, left to right** *In a Montreal hotel whirlpool relaxing before campaigning in 1974. This photo was taken through the hotel lobby window; Queen Elizabeth concentrates on the ceremonies at B.C. Place Stadium, March 9, 1983; Trudeau with Ronald Reagan, April 29, 1983.*

Above left *With Barbra Streisand at the National Arts Centre in Ottawa, January 28, 1970.* **Above right** *Cuban President Fidel Castro and Pierre and Margaret Trudeau look over a photo album during their state visit to Cuba, January, 1976. Castro presented Margaret with a collection of personal photographs, including this one, just hours before her ex-husband's funeral.* **Below, left to right** *John Lennon and Yoko Ono in Ottawa on their crusade for peace, December 24, 1969; Princess Diana and Prince Charles leave a state dinner, June 15, 1983.*

Above With Quebec Premier Rene Levesque (right), who is giving his trade-mark shrug, at the beginning of the second day of the Constitution Conference, September 9, 1980. **Right** With Jean Chretien, 1972.

Succession of power, **counter-clockwise from bottom,** *former Prime Minister Pearson and Trudeau discuss the Liberal Party leadership changeover in Ottawa in April, 1968. Trudeau had just succeeded Pearson as party leader; with Ed Broadbent and Joe Clark (right) after the leader's debate in 1979. Joe Clark won the 1979 election, narrowly; John Turner won the leadership of the Federal Liberal Party, June 16, 1984.*

Jacques Hebert's Eulogy

Facing page *Trudeau chats with Jean Marchand (standing, left) at the launching of Gerard Pelletier's book* Le Temps des choix *(Time for Choices) in Montreal, November, 1986. Known as the three "wise men," the friends entered federal politics the same year and arrived in Ottawa as* MPs *in 1965.*

Pierre Trudeau very much loved this thought of Aristotle: The principle of society is that its members be able, collectively and individually, to live life fully.

All his years as head of government, he pursued this goal with the tenacity we all knew in him. He was convinced it was necessary, above all, to help young people blossom. These last days, much has been said of his more spectacular works: the Constitution, the Charter of Rights and Freedoms, official languages and the rest. But we must also evoke his immense compassion for the youth of this country.

He never hesitated to place at the forefront programs aimed at young people, like the unique, audacious Opportunities for Youth, Canada World Youth, Katimavik—of which he still spoke to me with affection just 10 days before his death, in a voice barely audible, as if it were already coming from another world.

Tens of thousands of young people were deeply changed and live full and fruitful lives thanks to one or another of the things Pierre Trudeau did for youth—that voiceless minority that until then had never interested politicians.

One day in 1959, long before he entered politics, I asked him for help (as a lawyer) getting a young orphan out of the grip of the rotten system that then existed. An illegitimate orphan, one of Duplessis' orphans, as we said... Pierre Trudeau

threw himself heart and soul into this struggle that lasted long months, until this young 19-year-old victim could regain his freedom and dignity. One example among thousands of the generosity of this man.

When he was young and free, some called him a playboy, because he was seen occasionally on a ski hill or in a discotheque. Saturdays, maybe. But the rest of the week, his friends can testify, he worked doggedly at writing articles that would feed the Quiet Revolution and overturn conventional ideas.

He was one of the most ardent defenders of the young Quebec union movement, barely tolerated (in those days), and of civil liberties when they were battered. For those who admired him, Pierre Trudeau remains a hero and a giant, a sort of superman, proud, courageous, a knight of our era. A man of immense culture, uncommon intelligence placed at the service of Quebec and Canada, the province and the country for which he had a passion.

But those who had the privilege of being his friends remember a different Pierre Trudeau from the exalted, unpredictable, extraordinary person that the media describe. For his friends, Pierre Trudeau was above all a joyful companion, a human being of simplicity, of an infinite delicacy, generous, attentive—it may astonish those who never knew him and spoke of his arrogance. He had an exquisite sense of friendship.

That is why the illness and death of his friend Gerard Pelletier—our common friend—so deeply affected him. After the funeral, with a sigh, he murmured these words, rather incredible in such a discreet man: "I've just lost a bit of my soul."

The day we learned of his (Trudeau's) death, even if we had expected it, how many of us had the same feeling. A bit of ourselves had just left us forever.

Whether as friends or political foes, he profoundly marked us all, by forcing us to think, to question ourselves and debate ideas rather than feelings. Because of Pierre Trudeau we have become better human beings and Canada is now a more generous and caring country. As he once said, a country can be influential in the world by the size of its heart and the breadth of its mind. And this is the role Canada can play.

Among Pierre Trudeau's qualities, there is one on which everybody agrees. Until his last breath he was an admirable father who gave the best of himself to his children, when he could have let himself be distracted by the pressing needs of being prime minister.

He adored his three sons and his daughter. And with an infinite patience he transmitted to them his fundamental values—his love of culture and of nature, his sense of discipline.

When I think of Pierre Trudeau, I can't help seeing him surrounded by his three boys at various stages of their life, as in the numerous photographs that lined the walls of his office and home.

We can all be glad of one thing at least. He died in peace, lucid, serene, accepting his fate—happy and surrounded by Justin, Sacha and Margaret. How he deserved that final moment.

Goodbye old brother. Rest in peace. We continue to love you.

Excerpts from the eulogy to Pierre Trudeau by Jacques Hebert

Robert Fulford

The Contrarian Viewpoint

No one ever glowed with such promise. No one ever carried such vibrant hopes into the Prime Minister's Office. And no one ever disappointed Canada on such a grand scale.

Early in 1968, as Lester B. Pearson prepared to retire and the Liberal party planned its leadership convention, the idea that Pierre Trudeau might become prime minister sent a charge of political energy flowing across Canada. But the very idea seemed impossible to many of us. "Too good to be true," said Blair Fraser of *Maclean's*, the shrewdest political writer in Ottawa, as well as a friend and admirer of Trudeau's. It couldn't happen.

Trudeau was intelligent, attractive, articulate and imaginative. In the 1950s he had fought the repressive political machine of Maurice Duplessis, the Quebec premier. He was a civil libertarian, and a Quebecer who believed in Canada. In 1965 he had pulled up his roots in the New Democratic Party and planted himself among the Liberals so that he could serve in Parliament and help save the country from Quebec separatism. As Pearson's justice minister in 1967, he had expunged the archaic anti-homosexual law from the Criminal Code.

It was hard to imagine the powerbrokers of the Liberal party endorsing someone so original, so bright, so aloof, and so alien to the normal style of Canadian politics. A friend phoned to ask that I sign up with my Liberal riding association and vote to send Trudeau-committed delegates to Ottawa.

So I spent one evening as a Liberal, my first and last experience of party membership. I told my friend that though I didn't expect we could win, just getting Trudeau

Singing the national anthem at the 1968 Grey Cup game (Ottawa. vs. Calgary) in Toronto

a prominent place among the candidates would be worth the effort. My friend said no, we were going to win.

He was right. In that frantic and exciting spring, Trudeau embodied the spirit of the moment. The country was ready for new beginnings, even if we couldn't say what they should be. Canada was giddy with a fresh sense of nationhood, having just celebrated the centennial year at Expo '67, the magnificent world's fair in Trudeau's home town, Montreal. Young people were suddenly a larger force in politics and society than ever before; Trudeau, middle-aged but athletic, was (everyone agreed) young at heart. As the April leadership convention approached, the idea of a charming, totally bilingual French-Canadian federalist gathered national support, and by the time he defeated John Turner, Paul Martin Sr. and five others, his victory seemed entirely natural and almost inevitable. In the May election, the country gave him the parliamentary majority that had twice eluded the far more distinguished and experienced Pearson.

Trudeau came across as something of a movie star, the first such personality in our political history. If he was also sometimes silly, we could reassure ourselves that he was, after all, a constitutional lawyer, a former professor of law at the University of Montreal, and a friend of many of the country's leading intellectuals. It took some of us years to figure out that there was less to him than met the eye.

At the beginning, he did for Canadians what Ronald Reagan later did for Americans: He made us feel good about ourselves. Eventually he would make us feel bad—about ourselves and about him. He was as brilliant as his earliest reviews had suggested, but the flaws in his personality swiftly became evident. For one thing, he was more obsessed with personal power than anyone expected—much more than Pearson or Louis St. Laurent, his predecessors as Liberal leader. Having frowned in disapproval at conflicts among Pearson's ministers, he kept his own Cabinet on a short leash and made free discussion of issues a punishable offence. More important, he withdrew most of the power of the ministers and centralized all authority in his office and the Privy Council Office.

What he accomplished was a silent and entirely legal coup, and it took at least two years before many people outside Ottawa knew what he had done. By then it was 1970, and we were heading toward a new disillusionment: the discovery that our

Facing page *In Montreal, October 21, 1979*

much-admired civil libertarian did not believe in civil liberties for those who radically disagreed with him. In October, FLQ separatist terrorists kidnapped a British diplomat, James Cross, and then a Quebec Cabinet minister, Pierre Laporte. It seemed to many in Quebec and Ottawa that frighteningly large numbers of citizens were sympathetic to the terrorists.

Trudeau, apparently in a panic, invoked the War Measures Act, which imposed censorship on the media and gave the police arbitrary powers of arrest. More than 450 Quebecers, most of whom had committed no crime and were never charged with one, were rounded up and hauled off briefly to jail, where they were held incommunicado. Here was an act worse than anything Duplessis ever dreamt of committing.

Not long after, the murder of Laporte seemed to give legitimacy to Trudeau's actions, at least for the moment. But those of us who had so admired him in 1968 now realized that he believed in a principle when that principle was convenient; otherwise, he believed in power.

In foreign affairs, his record was equally dubious and untrue to his own past. The man who had fought the censorship of the Duplessis government never quite understood that the many dictatorships imposed by the Soviet Union were incomparably worse. In the 1970s, Trudeau showed no sympathy for the dissidents across eastern Europe who were fighting a long and lonely (and often apparently hopeless) battle against Moscow. He saw them as irresponsible agents of disorder who might disturb the world's delicate status quo. "He considered them thugs," a senior diplomat told me, after watching Trudeau's reactions over the years. To Canada's eternal shame, Trudeau expressed sympathy with the venomous General Wojciech Jaruzelski when the general imposed martial law on Poland in 1981, banned Solidarity and arrested union leaders. After fighting in the 1950s against uncaring elites, particularly on behalf of trade unions, Trudeau in power turned into the natural friend of despots—even Fidel Castro.

His charm, so evident at the beginning, soured early. He found it hard to work with people who challenged him—and he had no patience with those less bright than he. Condescension was the style of his conversation. He was usually the brightest person in the room, and he made sure everyone knew it. Ministers with independent reputations began drifting away. Two finance ministers left the Cabinet in

"Pierre Trudeau gave a phenomenal contribution to the national consciousness. He will be greatly missed."

quick succession, John Turner in 1975, Donald Macdonald in 1977. Eventually the Cabinet turned into a collection of mediocrities, and it became clear there was only one important Liberal in Ottawa. By comparison, Pearson's Cabinet shone with excellence.

The country had originally cast Trudeau as the mediator between Quebec and the rest, the man who would restore stability to government and let us all move on to more serious work. In this he failed miserably. He thought that making Canada nominally bilingual through the Official Languages Act would help French-Canadians to feel at home everywhere in the country, a vain hope—at least in the short term. Instead, separatism persisted.

Respectable separatism (separatism considered as a viable "option" at every level of society and in every region) is a legacy of the Trudeau years.

In Quebec, his theories lasted only as long as his power. When he retired in 1984 he left behind no Trudeau school of thought in the universities and no Trudeau faction in politics. It seemed to outsiders that Quebec conquered Ottawa in the Trudeau years, but within Quebec this made no noticeable difference. Quebec voters supported him so long as he was there, but when he left office they appeared anxious to forget everything he stood for. Today, even federalists seldom quote him, and provincial Liberals show no sign that he ever mattered. The Quebec Liberal party remains dominated by purely provisional Canadians, prepared to remain Canadian only if Ottawa and the other provinces somehow provide an acceptable deal. It remains an astonishing fact that in his own province, Trudeau's beliefs about the meaning of Canada were like water poured in the sand (as one of his academic critics, Reg Whitaker, put it).

Would national unity have been served better by a less ferociously combative and more conciliatory prime minister? We can never know, but we know for sure that his way didn't work. Apparently, he had no interest in speculating on why this was so. When I asked him about it, his answer was grim, brief and totally incurious: his enemies were wrong, and that was the end of it. Not the reasoned response of an intellectual.

At some point a horrible thought occurred to many people who had once admired him: He wasn't nearly as serious about his job as he needed to be.

"I was very young when he was prime minister . . . but his impact on my life and that of the country has been felt. I can only hope that other young people in Newfoundland and in Canada would remember him as an important figure in our history."

He was serious about creating a place of equality for French-Canadians, and about "patriating" the Constitution and entrenching the Charter of Rights and Freedoms. In his own terms, he was a success on the constitutional issue, even if he did infuriate the Quebec government. The Charter, his chief monument, has changed Canada by greatly enhancing the power of appeal court judges and altering the way laws are made: Legislatures today operate in the knowledge that in most cases they must conform to the Charter and its judicial interpreters. Whether this has made us more free, as it was intended to do, is debatable. Those of us who dislike the Charter (mostly non-lawyers) and those who passionately love it (mostly lawyers and rights-seeking groups) have almost stopped arguing about it. We know that it will be part of Canada far into the 21st century.

In the career of Trudeau, it remains a startling and incomprehensible anomaly. He was the most anti-American of all our Liberal prime ministers, but giving power over Parliament to the Supreme Court, and raising the court to the same level as the nine judges in Washington, did more to Americanize Canadian government than any other single act of the 20th century. Perhaps a Trudeau biographer will some-day explain this most baffling of his many contradictions.

But even if his motives were hard to understand, he remained firm to the end on the Constitution, as he did on bilingualism. On everything else, he was capricious. He worried intensely about the Third World one year and forgot about it the next. He developed the Third Option in trade and foreign policy (meaning closer ties with Europe), talked about it a lot, then absent-mindedly dropped it. He fought passionately against wage and price controls in the 1974 election, then abruptly made them law soon after being re-elected. He seems never to have been much interested in economics, and he hardly noticed that he was presiding over the drift into crippling permanent debt. He appears to have approved the National Energy Policy without even being aware that it would make Albertans and many others curse his name.

In his early years as prime minister he devalued the External Affairs Department, belittled the legacy of Pearson, and brought Canada's greatest period of diplomacy to a melancholy end. And then, toward the end of his time in office, he became the great avatar of peace and demanded that the diplomats organize his last strut on the

"Trudeau was the warmest, most sincere intellectual type of person who never made people feel lower than he was."

world stage, a global peace-seeking tour that in the end seemed more an empty gesture than a serious attempt to grapple with the issues of the Cold War.

But even those who spent much of their adult lives passionately disagreeing with him had to admit that in person he was supremely impressive. I last saw him in 1992, a few weeks before his 73rd birthday.

This was the time of the Charlottetown accord, and he was explaining to a private dinner of two dozen Torontonians why he was opposed to it. He spoke for 20 minutes, and made every second count. He used no notes, but forged ahead so confidently, and made his points so clearly, that he seemed to be reading from a teleprompter located behind his eyes. "I want to come back to that sixth point in a moment," he would say—and by God, five minutes later he would come back, would find his place again, and would nail the point with astonishing precision. He had been thinking of these issues for four decades and had absorbed them into the core of his being. We were over-hearing an internal conversation that stretched back to the middle of the 1950s.

In that room there were people who had long since grown tired of his cool rhetoric and in fact had privately decided that his smugness was insufferable. But at the end of this performance we knew we had been privileged to watch a great virtuoso of argument at the top of his artful, beguiling form.

Trudeau perfected the "lone gunslinger" style to match his steely-eyed glance.

Max Nemni

The Multicultural Legacy

In 1999, more than 15 years after he walked away from public life, Pierre Elliott Trudeau ranked third as the most admired Canadian, after Celine Dion and Wayne Gretzky. Should we be surprised? Not in the least. Through five election campaigns, numerous constitutional deals, a separatist referendum, and the first and only battle against a truly Canadian brand of political terrorism, Canadians watched a man of courage and conviction lead their country. They saw him as a true statesman.

Already in his intellectual days at *Cité Libre*, he expressed with uncanny lucidity the political task that lay ahead for the Canadian federation: "The die is cast in Canada: there are two main ethnic and linguistic groups; each is too strong and too deeply rooted in the past, too firmly bound to a mother culture, to be able to engulf the other. But if the two will collaborate at the hub of a truly pluralistic state, Canada could become the envied seat of a form of federalism that belongs to tomorrow's world." While always a foe of "the ridiculous and reactionary idea of national sovereignty," he also believed the nation was "the guardian of certain very positive qualities: a cultural heritage, a community awareness, historical continuity, a set of mores." He favoured measures enriching the cultural heritage of all Canadians. What worried him was the idea that the frontiers of an ethnic group and those of the state should coincide. This is precisely what he witnessed in Quebec with the 1962 "Masters in Our Own House" election of Jean Lesage, ushering in the Quiet Revolution. Two years later, noting that English-Canadian nationalism and the new Quebec nationalism were "on a collision course," he urged that reason, federalism and law become the foundations of the Canada of tomorrow. On this note he went to Ottawa.

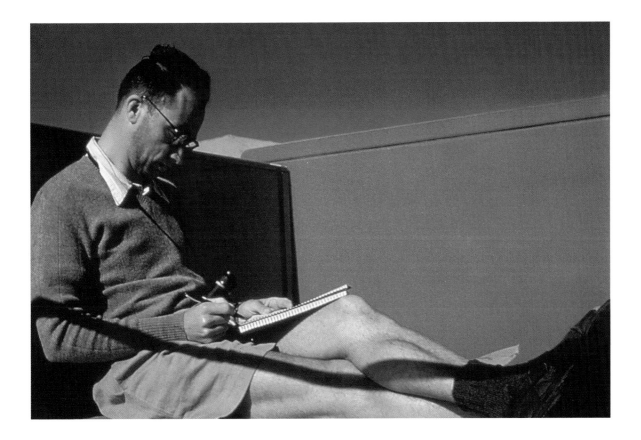

On a canoe trip on the Mackenzie River, 1956

Above *St. Jean Baptiste parade, Montreal, June 24, 1968*
Left *With former Quebec premier Robert Bourassa (centre)
at the funeral for Quebec Labour Minister
Pierre Laporte, 1970*

By entrenching bilingualism, Mr. Trudeau aimed at putting the two historic language communities on an equal footing, politically and constitutionally. The policy was never meant to make every Canadian bilingual. But to a great extent, Mr. Trudeau's policies have been realized, so much so a political career in Ottawa can hardly be envisaged without a sound knowledge of both languages. The recognition of both official languages as equal in juridical and political terms, and the entrenchment of language rights in the Constitution, have contributed to the creation of a distinct political nationality.

Multiculturalism was another pragmatic response to the reality of Canada. When Mr. Trudeau came to power, more than a third of Canadians were of neither English nor French origin. The 1982 constitutional reform acknowledges this by specifying the Charter must be interpreted "in a manner consistent with the preservation and enhancement of the multicultural heritage of Canadians." This has helped foster the strong patriotism of an increasingly multiethnic population.

The jewel in Mr. Trudeau's policies was the constitutional reform of 1982, and especially the Charter of Rights and Freedoms. Mr. Trudeau was not originally in favour of constitutional reforms, which he believed could only heighten divisions. However, he was always in favour of a bill of rights. He wrote in 1963: "I am increasingly coming to believe that Canadian federalism will reach full maturity only if we entrench in our Constitution a declaration of human rights and freedoms." Those who see in Mr. Trudeau's commitment a means of centralizing power in the hands of the federal government misunderstand him. The Charter gives primacy to individuals over their governments. Moreover, the Charter does not in any way touch upon the allocation of powers between the two levels of government. The only re-allocation of powers was in favour of the provinces, which gained greater control over natural resources.

Contrary to those who claim we have to live with the "status quo" because Mr. Trudeau did not accede to the demands of Quebec nationalists, in fact, under his leadership Canadian federalism has been renewed. Some may like these changes; others may hate them. One thing is certain: Steadfastly, Trudeau moved toward his objective and he reached it. Today's Canada is Trudeau's Canada. No wonder that he has secured a lasting place in the hearts and minds of so many Canadians.

Conrad Black

Trudeau's Federalism

When Pierre Trudeau became Prime Minister of Canada in 1968, the federal government had been led for 11 years by unilingual English-Canadians with few French-speaking collaborators capable of putting the federalist viewpoint in Quebec with any authority. The year before, General de Gaulle had committed his great prestige among the French-speaking people of the whole world to the cause of a sovereign Quebec, in his outrageous comments at Montreal. The Duplessis, Lesage and Johnson governments of Quebec had gained and claimed a large accretion of taxing power and general jurisdiction from the federal government over the previous 12 years. Trudeau attempted to refocus attention not on the distribution of powers between levels of government but on the rights of individuals. This was the beginning of the Canadian Charter of Rights and Freedoms, which, whatever its failings, was a considerable distraction to the Quebec separatists. By his far-reaching social programs, he made the federal government much more relevant to many Quebecers than it has been; extravagant, authoritarian and ineffectual though many of those programs were.

By packing the government with qualified French-Canadians and encouraging biculturalism throughout English-speaking Canada, Trudeau gave effect to the slogan with which he concluded his address to the convention that chose him as leader of the governing party in 1968: "Masters in our own house [maitres chez nous], but our house is all Canada." Thus, he turned the old Quebec nationalist slogan to federalist purposes and contended strenuously with Quebec nationalist leaders, especially Rene Levesque when he became premier of Quebec in 1976, for the political affections of the province. The federal opposition leaders whom he faced, Robert Stanfield and Joe Clark, were and remain sincere and conciliatory federalists. But neither could have been relied upon to defend the prerogatives of the federal state with the vigour or persuasiveness that Trudeau brought to the task. And in the FLQ Crisis of 1970, no one but Trudeau could have been relied upon to deal as effectively with the challenge to normal constitutional processes that followed the kidnapping of a British diplomat and the murder of Quebec's minister of labour.

Trudeau enters politics, 1965

Trudeau's leadership in the Quebec Independence Referendum Campaign of 1980, and especially his final speech of that campaign in the Paul Sauve Arena in Montreal, was masterful and could not have been replicated by any other federalist leader of any party.

There is room for extensive debate about many aspects of Trudeau's taxing and spending policies; his repatriation of the Constitution, including his acquiescence in a Charter of Rights that can be and at important times has been vacated by individual provincial governments, and about his promotion of the French fact throughout the country while failing to give any assistance to the non-French minority in Quebec who so faithfully re-elected him to Parliament. However, the ingenuity and conviction with which he pressed the federalist case, his natural qualities of leadership, physical and intellectual courage, panache and style, all made him federalism's irreplaceable leader at one of the most decisive periods in Canadian history.

Above *Trudeau and Britain's Prime Minister Margaret Thatcher outside 10 Downing Street, London, as delegation heads arrive for a working dinner prior to the Economic Summit, June 7, 1984*

Facing page *The Trudeaus attend a sugaring-off party at St. Joseph du Lac, Quebec, March 28, 1971.*

Roy Heenan's Eulogy

My colleague Jacques Hebert will address you in French. He or myself could render homage to Pierre Elliott Trudeau in both English or French and we would be understood by a majority of Canadians.

Like most Canadians I admired the prime minister—Pierre Elliott Trudeau. Our political leaders have eloquently testified of him as a leader and as a public man.

But I would like to talk to you about the private person who lived amongst us for the last 15 years. We came to know him as a warm and compassionate man invariably courteous to anyone he met. He was unassuming. He walked to work. He cared not for the trappings of power. One could not walk among the streets beside him without being stopped by somebody who wanted to shake his hand or say a few words to him. He was invariably cordial, patient and polite.

I have also learned the warmth of his friendship and I witnessed the depth of the love for his children. Justin, Sacha, Sarah—your father loved you and Mishu so very much. He was devoted to you. He was so proud of you. No one could ever go into his office or talk to him for a few minutes without realizing that you were never far from his thoughts.

The world knows that you have suffered a terrible loss but you will bear it

In his trademark buckskin jacket, 1995

secure in the certain knowledge of his great love for you. That must be your strength.

It has been said that Pierre Trudeau was aloof and distant. That is not the Pierre Trudeau I knew. On the contrary, he was caring, polite and kind, and he had such judgment. It was a privilege to discuss with him matters of the moment and witness his acute and analytical mind ready to engage in any discussion with enormous civility.

I will also remember the vigorous man who loved the outdoors. He loved skiing. His skiing style can only be described as daredevil. But he was afraid of no mountain and he delighted in the challenge. It was with great regret that he told me last April that this winter was the first winter in 75 years that he had not skied and he was sad.

He loved the oceans, swimming and scuba diving and, of course, canoeing. He wrote that the art of governing had some parallels with the art of canoeing. Sometimes you have to fight against the current. He never hesitated to do that.

I'm told that Pierre Elliott Trudeau died last Thursday. The man maybe, but his ideas live on. I speak not as a politician but as an ordinary citizen. Over the last few days, citizens by the tens of thousands have turned out to bear witness of their love and admiration for Pierre. We saw it in Ottawa on Parliament Hill. We saw it on the train that brought him back home to his beloved city. And we saw it again here in Montreal in the last two days.

And why? Why do the citizens respond so spontaneously. Because he was a remarkable leader? That's true but it's not because of that. It is because he created and articulated a vision of this country which resonates in the hearts and minds of millions of Canadians. He defended that vision both rationally and passionately both at home and abroad.

And what is that vision that is shared by so many? First, of peoples living together in harmony in a single state and that brother not be turned against brother.

Second, that we aspired to a just society—one that offers equality of opportunity. A vision of understanding of and charity towards others, particularly the less fortunate.

That the two cultures of Canada flourish and be nurtured across this great land. And that other cultures enrich us. That bilingualism is an asset, not a liability. And, of course, that the fundamental rights and freedoms be ensured and enshrined for all Canadians. This vision has changed forever the sense of ourselves as a society.

This is his legacy to us. This is the testament of Pierre Elliott Trudeau, who left it to all Canadian men and women that he loved so well. We will also remember that on a deeper and more personal level he challenged us all to be the very best that we could be. We have been touched by greatness. Today we say au revoir to Pierre and we bury the body. But the vision continues. The vision lives.

Trudeau's office in Montreal.

Sacha Trudeau's Reading

Facing page *Holding six-year-old Sacha during a tour of the ancient tombs Madein Saleh in Saudi Arabia on November 18, 1980*

I saw a tree
in the middle of the world;
it was very tall.

The tree grew taller and stronger,
until it reached the sky
and it could be seen from the very ends of the
earth.
Its foliage was beautiful, its fruit abundant,
in it was food for all.
For the wild animals it provided shade,
the birds of heaven nested in its branches,
all living creatures found their food on it.

I watched the visions passing through my head as I lay in bed:

Next, a Watchful One, a holy one, came down from heaven.
At the top of his voice he shouted:
Cut the tree down, lop off its branches,
strip off its leaves, throw away its fruit;
let the animals flee from its shelter
and the birds from its branches.

But leave the stump with its roots in the ground,
bound with hoops of iron and bronze,
in the grass of the countryside.
Let it be drenched by the dew of heaven
and have its lot with the animals, eating grass!

A reading from the fourth Book of Daniel

Left *Father and son during
a reception following
Sacha's graduation at
Canadian Forces Base in
1996. Sacha, 22, was an
officer of the Royal
Canadian Hussars, a
reserve regiment based
in Montreal.*
Facing page *Trudeau
greets his boys after
arriving home from a
foreign trip, 1983.*

Return to Private Life

Right *Casts his ballot in Montreal for the referendum on the package of constitutional changes, October 26, 1992. Trudeau came out publicly against the package early in the campaign.*

Below, left to right *Trudeau's last fishing trip was to New Brunswick, with his son Sacha, former Governor General Romeo LeBlanc and his son Dominic LeBlanc.*

Former Soviet Union President Mikhail Gorbachev says goodbye to Trudeau after a meeting in Montreal, March 29, 1993.

Facing page *Pierre and Margaret leave a memorial service for their son Michel in Montreal. Michel Trudeau drowned after being swept into a lake during an avalanche in British Columbia in 1998.*

Pierre Trudeau and Margaret Sinclair

Christie Blatchford

Margaret

Justin Trudeau had just finished his tremendous eulogy with a strangled cry of "Je t'aime, Papa." In his young man's suit, pearl grey shirt matching the tie, he walked to the casket, and laid there his dark shiny head.

Chin trembling now, he raised up his white face, already in need of another shave and surely already very dear to his countrymen, and he stood there, hard-won composure washing away in tears.

Less than a foot away, Margaret Trudeau hesitated, mother's heart propelling her to her oldest son, something wiser or harder telling her not to go to him, not now, not yet. She took a step forward. She raised an arm. She stopped. She stood still. The arm fell to her side.

She waited, and in a matter of seconds, he came to his seat, and to her, and she reached up to stroke his wet cheek with unbearable tenderness, a proud and tremulous smile on her beautiful face, and then the woman who was once Pierre Trudeau's child bride Maggie, and their two surviving sons, Justin and Sacha, were suddenly wrapped 'round one another, limbs entwined.

As a metaphor for the nation that nearly tears itself apart every decade, retreats from the dreadful precipice and then falls in love all over again, this awkward, graceful and fractured first family of Canada is as good and as true as it gets.

You see what Maggie has learned? And how those boys—as forever, it seems, they will be in the collective consciousness—have learned. Will the country?

God knows, the temptation is to borrow from the Book of Common Prayer, and say: Those whom Pierre Trudeau hath joined together, let no man put asunder.

At the grand Notre Dame Basilica, they were in the front row, in this order:

Justin, a 29-year-old school teacher in British Columbia; the gentle Maggie, 51, a second marriage behind her; Sacha, the second Christmas Day baby, a 27-year-old video journalist; Deborah Coyne, the shy constitutional lawyer who in 1991, when Mr. Trudeau was 72, gave birth to his only daughter, and beside her, Sarah, that blond daughter; and Mr. Trudeau's sister, Suzette Rouleau.

There was this small, slightly uncomfortable space between the groupings—Justin, Maggie and Sacha in a bunch at one end of the row; Ms. Coyne and Sarah, in her dark blue velvet dress, in the middle; Ms. Rouleau alone at the other end. How very Canadian that even in unity, these six also should have been apart, one a curious, but equal, distance from the other.

Well, Mr. Trudeau's vaunted inclusiveness was never meant to be smothering.

Perhaps the lesson to take is that they were content to be linked in this fashion, as everywhere else, Canadians were on the last day of the long goodbye to their 15th prime minister.

Inside the great church, the Cuban President Fidel Castro sat in the same row as former U.S. president Jimmy Carter. Federal Tory leader Joe Clark was next to former Liberal prime minister John Turner. Separatists were cheek by jowl with ardent federalists.

In this high-security section, reserved for special guests and dignitaries, sat a man in a hockey jacket and a woman in a plaid lumberjack's shirt, clearly invited, but who were they? The legendary singer-songwriter Leonard Cohen was an honorary pallbearer. The native leader Matthew Coon-Come and more former Manitoba premiers than seems possible were among political movers and foreign leaders and royalty. The actress Margot Kidder, one of the famous women Mr. Trudeau took as lovers, after his marriage ended, was there. In this atmosphere, it was almost surprising that another of them, Barbra Streisand, didn't come along to sing a song.

Outside, warm applause from the crowds along Rue Notre Dame had followed the cortège as it travelled the few blocks from Montreal City Hall to the church. So, for the second consecutive day, in the heart of French Canada, did people break into "O Canada," reducing themselves and others, who could not sing let alone speak, to tears.

Mr. Trudeau's casket moved along on a wave of these sounds—the anthem, the steady swell of clapping, the noise of a thousand conversations carried on in the two founding languages and the dozens of others whose members have since joined the Canadian federation.

These people had waited in line for hours, made new friends, taken turns buying rounds of coffee from the charming patisserie down the road, talked politics, reminisced about the former prime minister that a remarkable number of them had actually met, in person. Roman Rockcliffe, a 29-year-old who had driven in from Oakville, Ontario, was one of them.

In 1995, on a cross-Canada canoeing trip to raise money for AIDS research, he and a young British Columbia man named Frank Wolf arrived in Montreal. A powerful Liberal friend in Toronto had suggested they call Mr. Trudeau if they needed help.

They were desperate for media attention, and more desperate for a way to avoid a painful two-day portage across the St. Lawrence. Mr. Rockcliffe phoned Mr. Trudeau's assistant, was put right through to him, and the two men were invited to lunch in the building of the law office where Mr. Trudeau was working.

Mr. Rockcliffe mentioned the publicity need first, and suggested perhaps, if Mr. Trudeau were to paddle with them one day, the press would come.

"Aaaah," said Mr. Trudeau with a slow smile. "The media and I, we've had our time together."

But on the other matter, he made a phone call, and the next morning, when Mr. Rockcliffe knocked on the door of the gatekeeper of the St. Lawrence Seaway, where canoes are not allowed, the lockmaster who answered told them: "If it's OK with Mr. Trudeau, it's OK with me." And away they went.

This day would have been OK with Mr. Trudeau, and no accident, for Justin and Sacha were intimately involved in its planning, and the service was filled with

"Although I was but a babe and young child during your prime ministry, your name and legacy would catch up to me many years later. I wish you eternal peace and give great thanks for what you did for our country. I wish I could have been older during your time in Parliament."

generous gestures, not the least of which came early in Justin's eulogy, when he told a wonderful story, of how, at the age of six, he was taken to the North Pole on his first official trip.

He went, he said, with his dad and "my grandpa Sinclair." In this way, by including his mother's father, James, including Maggie herself.

Maggie is at the centre of so much of it.

She was 18 years old when she met the dashing prime minister who would become her first husband. She was a free, long-legged, wild spirit then, as so many young women were in the early 1970s, and really starkly lovely. It is the memory of her—trusting the press with her heart, melting the natural public reserve of her much older husband, the two of them dancing—which has stayed with me all these years, more even than that of Mr. Trudeau himself.

Was she foolish on occasion? Of course she was. Was she sometimes indiscreet? She was. Who wasn't then? What many Canadians remember from this time are the photographs of her at that den of iniquity, Studio 54 in New York City, the stories of that much-publicized frolic with the Rolling Stones, the careless poses, the rambling interviews in which she sounded silly. She acquired a reputation for liking attention when, in fact, that the camera was drawn to her was hardly her fault: She was lovely.

In fact, as one of my friends noted this week, Maggie always played by the rules, all the rules, in one central area of her life: She gave Mr. Trudeau his reason to live—his three reasons, actually, Justin, Sacha and Michel—and even after their divorce in 1984, she remained a steadfast parent.

Yet over the years, this label stuck.

Maggie Trudeau has led, in fact, a reasonably private life since she and Mr. Trudeau parted, but she would pop back into the news periodically, still photogenic, still too gabby, and in these last two years, as first Michel was killed so horribly in an avalanche in British Columbia and then the death watch began for Mr. Trudeau, she was centre stage again, and the press corps turned its cruel eye on her again, pronouncing her, early on, as the same old drama queen.

In truth, she had grown immeasurably.

When her former husband's body was first brought to the Uplands military base

"Thanks for the great memories, you left the country a much better place."

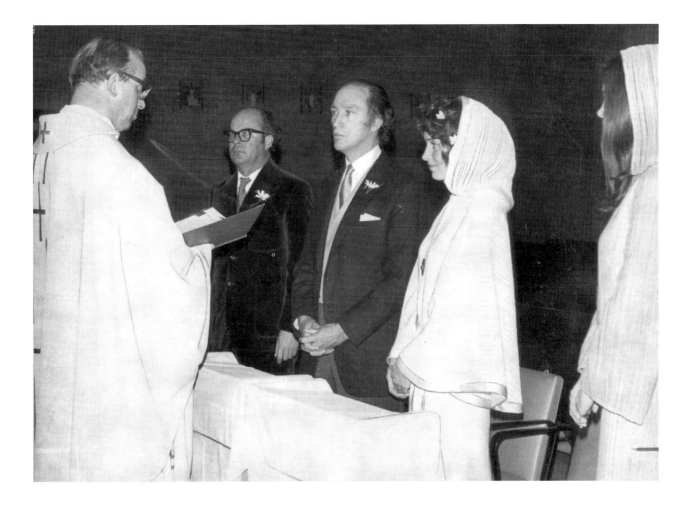

Above *Maggie and Pierre's wedding, Vancouver, March 4,*
1971 (left) John Kels, Charles Trudeau (Best Man), Pierre
Trudeau, Margaret Sinclair and Rosalind Sinclair
Right *Showered with good wishes on their wedding day*

preparatory prior to the lying-in-state at Parliament Hill, it was Maggie who was there, more than an hour early, all alone. She embraced Justin and Sacha, she held it together until she was in the car that took her back to town.

There, thinking it safe to cry, she fell apart; the next day, there was a news story quoting the unnamed driver that her collapse had not been "a pleasant sight." The tone was set: She should not cry; she should cry; she should cry prettily.

She showed up for a private visit at the Parliament Buildings, and was of course photographed. When Mr. Trudeau's body was moved to the funeral train that would take him home to Montreal, Maggie briefly emerged at the Centennial Flame, thanked some of the tens of thousands who had come for coming, and was promptly felled—quite literally; she dropped to her knees—when a television reporter asked if this burden was made harder by the fact it was also Michel's birthday. The rumour mill went into overdrive: Why wasn't she on that train, with the boys and Mr. Trudeau's friends?

Well, this is how she conducted herself on that day.

She walked into Notre Dame like a soldier, ramrod straight, eyes forward. She wore a simple black dress, a pearl choker on her slim neck. She looked like a million bucks.

As she entered the cathedral, her quavering, radiant smile appeared as she saw familiar faces, among them President Castro, who is said to have been much taken with her in those long-ago days when her husband defied the Americans and established relations with Cuba, and who on this day sat behind her in the row with former U.S. president Jimmy Carter.

She sat between her kids, each of them wearing a red rose, like their dad always did, in their lapels.

She held on to Sacha's hand as they took their seats.

She looked up once, into the bright television lights above her. She blinked.

Early on, as the first kind words about Mr. Trudeau were said, the first prayers murmured, she bit her lip hard, clearly trying not to cry.

Several times she appeared lost in memory; her head tilted up, eyes shut. Sometimes, she gently shook her head and, because of her prominent cheekbones, it was difficult to know if she was smiling or weeping, only that her mouth had opened wide, in happiness or distress.

When Sacha rose to give his reading, in a strong voice, she could not take her eyes off

him; she glowed with the wonder of a parent who is seeing, in one stellar instant, what the child has become.

She bowed her head and wept and, for the first time, took out a handkerchief that was precisely the colour of Mr. Trudeau's famous red rose.

When Sacha returned to his seat, she wrapped an arm around his shoulders and touched his arm. She rubbed his back, as surely as she had done a thousand times before. She rested her head on his shoulder.

She was soon rolling the red hankie in her hands. She and the boys cried together, in sequence; one would start, then another would begin.

She put her head on Justin's shoulder, and for a few seconds, they smiled at one another.

In her seat, almost imperceptibly, she began to quietly rock back and forth.

Clockwise from left, Justin, Margaret and Sacha Trudeau, Deborah Coyne, Romeo Leblanc, and Cuban President Fidel Castro watch as Cardinal Turcotte blesses the casket during the state funeral for Pierre Trudeau, Tuesday, Oct. 3, 2000, in Montreal.

RESERVED
RÉSERVÉ

Soon, tears were streaming down her face. Soon, the hankie was a sodden ball.

Justin saw this, put his around her, and at that, her head fell again on to the curve of his neck. She stayed like this a few more seconds, then lifted her face, and she was smiling at him, a smile of unbearable tenderness, and then Justin began to weep.

She leaned on one, then the other.

She reached a slim arm back behind her, to President Castro, and for a moment, he folded her hand into his.

Another time, she reached back for Jimmy Carter. He bent forward, whispered in her ear, and before she could take back her hand, he had kissed it.

She, Justin and Sacha were the first to take communion; when they sat down again, as the others joined in, the three of them talked quietly together, heads bent.

The eulogies followed, Roy Heenan, the chairman of Mr. Trudeau's law firm first, his colleague Jacques Hebert second.

"Lots of love and prayers, God bless you always."

One by one, Mr. Heenan in English, Mr. Hebert in French, they spoke of Mr. Trudeau the man, the father, and of how his much-perceived reserve did not exist in private. By the time Mr. Heenan told the story of how, last April, Mr. Trudeau confessed that for the first time in 75 years, he would not be skiing the next winter, and that it made him terribly sad, Maggie and Justin were holding hands. "I am told Mr. Trudeau died last Thursday," Mr. Heenan said. "But his ideas live on."

By the time Mr. Hebert, in his almost courtly French, was winding to a close, Maggie and Justin were sobbing in one another's arms.

Justin then walked to the front of the magnificent building. He resembles both parents, has Magic Marker eyebrows over piercing intelligent eyes, a wide, wide smile.

It began as a young man's speech. Only a young man, a novice at these occasions, would have opened with: "Friends, Romans, countrymen."

But the young Trudeaus are cut from their daddy's cloth, and soon the speech had turned profound, touching, overwhelmingly loving.

He spoke as well as his father ever had. He spoke of how Mr. Trudeau had loved his children, adored them, doted on them, but never indulged them. He spoke of the immense job they had, having to live up to a man of this stature, but then grinned and said, "He gave us a lot of tools." He's an honest kid; the legacy is immense, but he and Sacha (and, once, Michel) are not unequipped.

He told the congregation of his father's love, and belief, in every single Canadian, and then, a difficult moment, he said with every rose, every card, every outstretched hand, every pirouette these last five days, Canadians had given their love back to him and Sacha, and how very much this had meant.

His father, he said, would not be coming back, not this time, as he had for the Charlottetown accord and for Meech Lake. "It's up to us, all of us, now."

Throughout, Maggie Trudeau's eyes did not leave her son. She was transfixed, she glowed from within, she was utterly stricken all at once.

Then came that scene of tremendous, touching awkwardness, Justin weeping at the casket, his mother hovering, unsure. It may be that what held her back was nothing more than recognition that Justin must endure this moment by himself. God help me, I hope it wasn't that she feared intruding, or that if she grasped him to her, it would be misinterpreted.

Whatever her reasons, she stopped herself from going to him, and stood still. In the end, she had done the improbable, and turned that most public of funerals, the state funeral for a beloved leader, into a private one.

The organist thundered out "O Canada."

Everywhere, people sobbed, in the balconies, on the floor, outside the church. Never has a collection of Canadians more longed to sing their anthem, and never have they been so without voice.

The Mounties hoisted the casket they have carried for five full days on to their shoulders once again.

Dozens and dozens of white-robed priests followed, like a flock of birds.

Justin Trudeau gathered the pages of his speech—he is in more ways than one his father's careful, thinking child—and he and Sacha took their place in line, walking together.

Margaret Trudeau sought the arm of her former sister-in-law, Suzette Rouleau, and, whispering to the older woman, walked behind her sons.

Behind them came the quiet fair-haired Deborah Coyne and Pierre Trudeau's only daughter.

As goes the strange, wonderful family, apart and together both, so goes Canada.

Margaret Trudeau tests the diving board during a break in the election campaign in Penticton,

British Columbia, June 13, 1974.

Roy MacGregor

The Streets of Montreal

Of all the thousands and thousands who came to pay respects, he might have appreciated her the most.

Fifteen years old—born, he would note, a year after he had retired from politics and entered what is oblivion for most others—she came bearing stolen flowers and sat, Indian style, on the cobblestones in the square to the front of the church where far older and far more important people had been invited to say farewell to Pierre Elliott Trudeau.

She carried impatiens, the perfect flower for youth, orange ones plucked from a city flower pot far down the street from Notre Dame Basilica. She wore a dark peasant's skirt and carried a backpack stitched with advocacy buttons: Free Tibet, A Woman's Right to Choose, and even one amidst the anti-smoking and organic gardening messages that said, simply, Bite Me.

He would have loved that. Might even have used it had it been around when he was prime minister of the country she will inherit.

Rebecca Rosen was skipping school to say goodbye to a man she had never met but to whom she felt a natural and strong kinship. With her friends Alexandra Sterner and Eliza Urwin, all 15 and all Grade 10 students at Montreal's high school for fine arts, she had come hoping to fit into the huge church for the funeral only to be denied, like so many other hopefuls, by pressing demand and those who were already lined up as dawn broke.

They stayed anyway, three young women sitting beneath a beech tree, while the funeral mass bounced and echoed around the tall buildings surrounding the Basilica. They listened to the music, the priests, and in silence as Justin Trudeau spoke so

wonderfully of what it was like to know Pierre Trudeau as only his sons could.

Rebecca and Alexandra and Eliza had never known the man the son was speaking of in any other manner apart from family talk and history lessons. Their parents had greatly admired him and still greatly admire him. Their teachers had explained him and, presumably, will be explaining him for decades to come. But still these three very young women felt they knew him almost as a friend, a man old enough to be their father or grandfather or even great-grandfather, yet curiously young enough, through most of his 80 years, to have sat here with his legs crossed and talked about Tibet and passionate causes and those matters that make a life worth living.

"He had a moral code," said Rebecca, her head bowed shyly. "When he believed in something, he believed in it all the way."

He would have liked her saying that. He might have told her never to lose that spunk, to "take nothing for granted," as Justin Trudeau told the gathering, to stick to your guns, even if that means being against guns, and to make sure—as retired senator Jacques Hebert was reminding the gathering in a fractured, echoing voice— you "live life to the fullest." That, they believe, is what he did, and that's exactly what they plan to do with the decades that stretch out before them.

The Funeral

Above *John Turner, Joe Clark, Prince Andrew.* **Above right** *Senator Keith Davey, known as the "rainmaker" for his work running Trudeau's political campaigns.* **Right** *Leonard Cohen*

Clockwise from left *Sarah Coyne; Margaret with Trudeau's sister, Suzette Rouleau, his daughter,*
Sarah Coyne and Sarah's mother, Deborah Coyne in the background; mother and son.

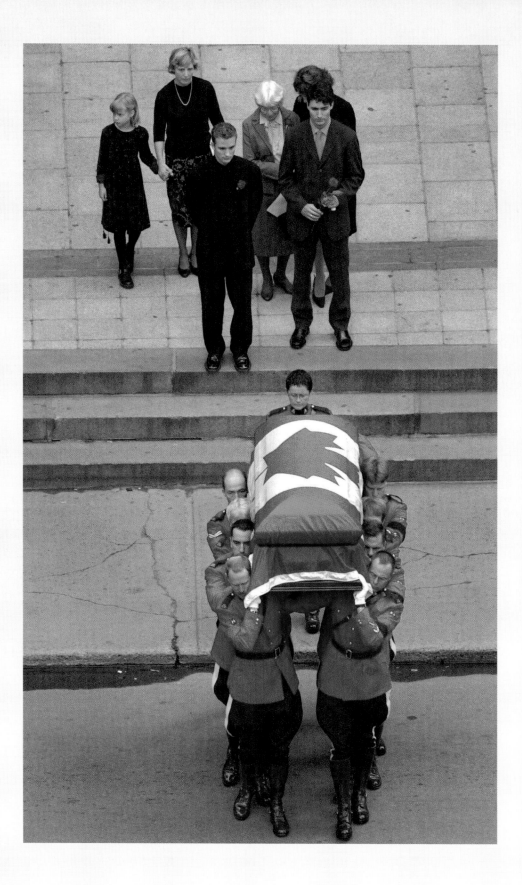

Above *Front row, from left, daughter Sarah Coyne and her mother Deborah, sons Sacha and Justin, sister Suzette Rouleau, former wife Margaret Trudeau-Kemper. Behind the family are Fidel Castro (right) and Jimmy Carter (left). Prime Minister Jean Chretien and his wife Aline are at far rear, centre.*